Leadership365

An All Inclusive Manual for Developing a Student Leadership Team

Table of Contents

Section One:

Introducing Leadership 365

Introduction

LeaderTreks is challenging the local church to make leadership development a core of student ministry. After talking with youth pastors all over the country about what they need in order to develop student leaders, we saw a unique need for a year-round curriculum that trains student leaders. More than a special summer emphasis or weekend retreat, Leadership 365 prioritizes leadership in your student ministry all year long.

This resource provides two semesters of critical lessons in leadership development. In two semesters, your team will learn the essentials of who leaders are and what leaders do. Because we believe that leaders are made, not born, we are committed to teaching principles of leadership that can be learned.

What Will Students Learn?

Semester One focuses on the reasons why studying leadership is important and centers on developing the character and attitudes of a leader. Students may be familiar with character traits like humility and compassion-but have they studied these traits in the context of leadership? Leaders lead from the heart. Before students will know what to do as a leader, they need to develop a foundation of godly character traits as they relate to leadership.

Semester Two focuses on the responsibilities and tasks of a leader. By studying concepts like navigating obstacles, charting a course and maintaining team focus, students will begin to acquire specific skills in the leadership arena. Through specific activities and initiatives, students will actually begin implementing these skills right away in a team setting.

How Does It Work?

We have isolated a different facet of leadership each week and packaged it with illustrations and learning activities that communicate truth in a student-friendly way. As a bonus, Leadership 365 includes several helpful articles tailored for adults with helpful and specific insights into how to create, manage and effectively utilize a student leadership team.

Each lesson easily fits a 60-90 minute timeframe. Lesson features include:

- Introduction: introduces the goals of the lesson

- Going Public: an intriguing question to kick off your study that requires students to "go public" about their own personal experience with a certain truth

- Getting Focused: an illustration or quote to probe the topic

- Growing Deeper: scriptural study

- Summary: recap of the lesson in a student-friendly one-page sheet

God's plan in building His Kingdom requires fully developed student leaders who are ready to assume real leadership roles. Leadership 365 provides exactly what you need to make this goal a reality in your student ministry week after week.

Student Leader's Companion Guide

We have also included a companion guide for students. The Leadership 365 Student Guide includes session notes for each of the sixteen teaching lessons as well as a planning journal.

This planning journal will be a great resource for your students as you release them to lead. It answers the question of every willing student leader: "What do I do now?" By following the LeaderTreks 5 Tasks of a Leader, your students will learn how to create a plan to see projects through to completion. This becomes a repeatable process that encourages student leaders to solve problems and complete tasks as a team. The journal includes sections on each of the 5 tasks:

1. Determine the scope and goals of the project. One of the greatest challenges of being a leader is seeing the future. Leaders must be able to set the boundaries of a project and determine goals to ensure the project will be completed with excellence.

2. Calculate the people and resources needed to complete the project. Leaders must put the right people in the right positions in order for a team to perform at maximum potential. Leaders must also provide the resources to complete projects whether that includes money, materials, or other necessities.

3. Cast the vision. A clearly communicated vision can change everything. If leaders are able to articulate their vision, no obstacle will stand in the way of their mission.

4. Navigate the obstacles. Leaders need to think about what is coming next and deal with problems before those issues sabotage a project. Leaders also need to deal with conflict between personalities and establish healthy environments.

5. Evaluate the performance. Leaders need to ask, "How can we do this better?" Consistent, honest evaluation is the leader's tool prompting growth in followers ensuring excellence in all that his or her team does.

By utilizing this simple system, you can enable your students to lead in new ways. Be sure to get the most out of Leadership 365 with these effective resources.

An Open Letter to Potential Student Leaders:

God's plan in building His Kingdom requires fully developed student leaders ready to assume real leadership roles right now. Students are not merely the "leaders of tomorrow." God wants to use student leaders like you today. God uses leaders to change the world, and He will use you to impact the Kingdom wherever you are.

The pursuit of leadership is a lifelong endeavor. Each day new opportunities will arise for you to exercise leadership skills. As you gain knowledge and experience you will learn more about what it means to be a leader. Remember, the best leaders are learners.

Jesus warned us to count the cost before we begin anything. So, remember:

Leadership is about tough decisions. *It's about making the best use of people and resources, setting good goals and evaluating the progress. The success of a leader can be measured by the decisions that he or she makes. These decisions are never easy, but always significant. Learning leadership principles, combined with real-life leadership experience, will help you make better leadership decisions.*

Leadership requires you to act. *When the chance comes to stand for the truth no matter the cost, true leaders are the first to rise to the challenge. True leaders are defined by godly character that allows them to meet whatever challenges they face.*

Leadership means sacrifice. *It is a sacrifice to take up the mantle of leadership. It is hard work. Leaders are exposed to criticism and rejection. It is much safer to remain on the sidelines, away from the scrutiny that leadership brings. Leadership may not make you popular, but it will make you strong.*

Leadership requires taking risks. *Some student leaders are worried about making mistakes. They are so focused on doing things right that they are unwilling to take a risk. To be a leader is to be a risk-taker with big dreams.*

Leadership depends on goals. *To be a big dreamer you need to set goals. Goals are a map to the life that God has always wanted you to have. Too many people go through life simply allowing things to happen to them and never fulfilling any of their dreams.*

Our hope for you is that Leadership 365 will be a year of lessons you never forget in your pursuit of what it means to be a leader. By applying the principles you will learn this year, you can impact your world for God's Kingdom—now! Be prepared for difficult challenges and tough times, but know that the sacrifice is worth it. God has big plans for you. You need to be ready to lead.

Section Two:
Strategies for Developing a High-Performance Student Leadership Program

Strategies for Developing a High-Performance Student Leadership Program

The hardest part of any new project is starting. This is also the biggest obstacle to starting a student leadership team. Momentum is not your friend in the beginning. You have lots of decisions to make and a few challenges to face. How you choose to start this new endeavor will greatly affect the outcome in your students' lives.

At LeaderTreks, we always prefer to start with the end in mind. If you know where you want to go, you can create a plan to reach your destination. Conversely, if you don't nail down your desired outcome, you may have trouble knowing what to do next. Knowing your end goal from day one will keep you on track and prevent many mistakes along the way.

Let's get started by examining a simple question: **Why do you want to start a student leadership team?** The answer to this question is vital. You need to know why you are investing your time and resources into student leadership so that you can measure the outcome, defend your program and unleash the potential of your student leaders. Will your student leaders help you in the day-to-day planning and implementation of your student ministry? Are you hoping to develop leadership skills in the lives of your students? Do you just want an excuse to work with the best students in your ministry more often? There is no right answer here. However, your answer will determine how you proceed.

Take some time right now and write down your top three to five reasons for starting your student leadership team.

1.

2.

3.

4.

5.

Now that you have the end in mind, how do you start?

Starting a Student Leadership Team

Owners vs. Attendees

A great place to start thinking about student leadership is examining how your students view the youth ministry. Do your students see their youth group as a ministry of the church to students or as the ministry of the students to their world? The question is an important one because it's the difference between just attending and being owners. Owners don't walk away. They have an investment, a stake in the goal. Just because they have graduated from high school doesn't change anything. Mere attendees buy a ticket and hope for a fun event. They don't see anything for themselves after graduation, so they walk.

So much is being said about students dropping out of church. Many are leaving at the end of high school and not returning until their mid 20s or later. The emergent leaders' movement is working hard on solutions the church can use to invite this generation back. The question youth workers must ask is, "Why did they leave in the first place?" It's not a matter of placing blame. We simply must know what is affecting these students and what our ministries can do to stop it from happening.

For a long time, youth ministry focused on entertaining students, having fun and liking the youth pastor. The theory was that if they had fun and liked the youth pastor, they would come. This short-sighted thinking communicated the wrong message to students that they are attendees not owners. Today is a new day. Many youth groups are now moving away from the entertainment model and heading towards student leadership.

Student ministries need to make owners of students. The best way to do this is to start a student leadership team. A student leadership team will allow students to set goals, resource projects, cast vision, rally the troops, lead ministries and be responsible for the success or failure of the group. Leadership teams have the potential to transform students' thinking. Where they once thought of themselves as participants in the plans of the youth pastor, they now can see themselves as the leaders of the ministry, the owners. This change in thinking has more power to capture hearts of students than entertainment ever could.

When a student leadership team is run well it will:

1. Not be for every student in your youth group-(it will be selective)

2. Require students to meet a standard of behavior for application

3. Meet on a regular basis

4. Study leadership principles

5. Have students in real, important leadership roles

6. Allow students to make decisions without interference from adults

7. Force students to face consequences of their decisions

8. Help students see themselves as the owners of their youth group

9. Have adult facilitators who are passionate about student leaders

10. Challenge students to do the impossible

Student leadership development is the key to seeing transformational change in students. Leadership will help unlock the potential of your students. Now that you are committing yourself to student leadership, you will soon see some of these amazing results. If you are realizing that you have merely attendees, not owners, now is the time for a change. It is the key to turning students into owners of the church and thus into long term members of the family of God.

Developing a Plan for Student Leadership

Students who are eager to sign-up to be on a leadership team may not be the leaders you want. Leadership is more than just being on another team at church. Leadership requires confrontation, problem solving and difficult decisions. Too often students think being a part of the leadership team means hanging out with the youth pastor and deciding what cool things the group will do. They seldom count the cost of leadership and can't be found when tough decisions need to be made.

Leadership teams in youth groups are a great idea. This leads some youth workers to think that if it's a great idea, why not get everyone on the team? This is the problem: we often select the team members before we have decided what the focus of the leadership team will be. If the leadership team is just about helping the youth pastor with logistics he or she doesn't want to do, put anyone on the team. However, if the team is about creating a strategic plan, casting a vision and execution then it requires that you select team members based on maturity, past performance, character and spiritual development.

Action step 1: Determine the focus and purpose of the leadership team. Meet with your adult team and brainstorm the purpose of a student leadership team. Start with the results: what do you want to see happen and how will your youth group look if you had an effective student leadership team? Then work backwards. To make these results happen, what leadership training will we need and what kind of projects can we turn over to students?

What is the focus and purpose of my leadership team?

Action step 2: Calculate what kind of students would be right for the leadership team you have created. Warning: don't just get "good students." Look outside the church box and see if a real leadership experience might be right for students that are disconnected in some way. Develop a good application*. This will help you and your staff understand the character and qualifications of the students that are applying. (*sample application is in the next section)

What students naturally come to mind when you think of student leaders?

Take it a step beyond the obvious. Where would you look for student leaders if you were looking outside the box?

Action step 3: Cast the vision with your whole youth group; let everyone know what the focus of the leadership team will be and what the standards of qualification are.

What is the vision of your student leadership team? Note some ideas here:

What do you anticipate will be the response to your vision?

Action step 4: Navigate the obstacles with students and parents. Understand that students and parents will want to know more about the qualifications and how the team members will be chosen. Be upfront and share with everyone the process you and your team have experienced to get to this point. Describe the results you are seeking. Be open yet firm; the long term success of this team will be determined by how you start.

What potential obstacles will you face?

Action step 5: Evaluate the progress. Once the applications start coming in, check to see that the applicants understand your focus and purpose. Interview students if need be. Keep meeting with your adult team and ask, "What can we do better?" The greatest pitfall to starting a leadership team might be allowing the process to get out of control. Slow down and think about the desired outcomes before you launch this program. Then find the right students who fit the focus of the team. By carefully creating a plan, your chances for success greatly increase.

Return to this section after you are a few miles down the road of starting your student leadership program. What have you done well? What areas need improvement? What unanticipated problems have you encountered? What are you learning?

Choosing the Right Students

Choosing the right students for your leadership team is obviously important to the success of your program. Having the wrong students will derail the team even before it gets started. Even though it may appear obvious, selecting the right students could be harder than it seems.

Getting students interested in leadership is the first step. There are many reasons why students may be reluctant to be involved. They may misunderstand what leadership is and what it requires. They may have a negative view of student leaders from bad experiences at school or on sports teams. They may be afraid of the increased responsibility that leadership brings. You will need to address the fears of the students as you introduce the leadership team concept to them. If you fail to do this, you may not capture the best students in your ministry.

If you find that there aren't enough students in your ministry who are interested in leadership, you may want to try a different approach. Introduce them to the idea by teaching your entire group what biblical leadership is all about.* By holding off until students understand leadership, you will have a much better chance of success for your leadership team. If you find that key students aren't excited about the leadership team, consider meeting with them one-on-one. In a personal setting, your can discover the cause of their reluctance toward leadership. Even if they still don't want to be on the team, their support will help the team be more successful.

LeaderTreks offers great small and large group resources to help students understand leadership and discover their own leadership gifts.

The Application Process

The best way to ensure that you find the right students is to have an application process.

An application process will help in several important ways. First, it conveys the importance and value of student leadership. By merely filling out an application, students will begin to understand the cost required to be a leader. It also allows you, your staff and some select parents to control who becomes part of the student leadership team. Allowing your students to vote in their own leaders or "taking anyone who signs up" takes away your power of selection. An application also gives you a chance to communicate the requirements of student leadership to anyone who is interested before they ever become part of the team. Setting the expectations early can alleviate many problems later on.

Many ideas can be incorporated into your application for your student leadership team. A good application would include expectations and requirements of student leaders, information on the time need to participate, areas to discuss personal spiritual growth and questions to determine students' motivation for student leadership. Be sure to tailor the student leader application to your environment and to the level of commitment that you are requiring from your students. If it's a short term commitment, the application might only be one page long. For a more intense program, you may require an application of several pages and request references. You will find a sample reference sheet, too, in this section. Think through your objectives and adjust your application accordingly.

Follow up the application with an interview process. The interview will give you a chance to address any concerns you have with the students that are applying. You can also make the expectations clear for them so they can make a good decision about being involved. This is another great time to get key parents or volunteers involved. Using their input you will be able to choose the best students and hopefully avoid the mistake of picking the wrong students.

You may also want to consider having all of your student leaders sign a leader's covenant. This covenant will make clear the responsibilities of being a student leader. A good covenant will ask students to commit to living a Godly lifestyle, be teachable, and attend all of the leadership meetings. Another benefit of the covenant is accountability. If you have students on the team who fail to live up to their responsibilities you can remind them of the covenant. They then have the choice to either change their ways or leave the team. On the following pages you will find both a sample application and covenant.

Student Leader Application Sample

You have a unique opportunity to play a key role in the success of our ministry. As a member of the student leadership team you will help cast vision for how the ministry should grow/change. You will also plan and implement a number of different events. Above all, you will grow deeper in your relationship with Christ and will be equipped with leadership skills that will help you lead not only in our ministry but in the church as a whole. This will not be an easy task. It will require your time, your heart and your commitment.

Expectations for Student Leaders

- Active pursuit of the life Jesus Christ calls us to live.
- Desire to impact the lives of others for Christ.
- Willingness to learn from students and staff who have gone before you.
- Full commitment and regular attendance at student leader meetings.
- Love and care for other members of the team.
- Enthusiasm in pursuit of leadership in the church.

Important Dates:

- July 15 - Applications Available
- July 31 - Applications Due
- August 1-5 - Phone or Face-to-Face Interviews
- August 10 - Student Leaders Selection
- August 20-22 - First Student Leader Meeting/Fall Training
- September 5 - Regular Bi-monthly Meetings Begin
- January 5-6 - Winter Training
- March 12-19 - Student Leader Wilderness Trip

Application for Student Leadership Team:

Name:

Grade/School:

Address: _____

City:_____ State:_____ Zip Code: _____

Phone (s): _____ Email: _____

Other commitments during the school year:

Describe your relationship with Jesus Christ. (250 words)

What one thing has God taught you recently?

How long have you been attending the church? How are you involved?

What makes someone a leader?

What one thing would you like to tackle as a leader in this ministry?

What one thing are you passionate about?

References

Three references are required. One from each of the following areas:

- Church - An adult volunteer in the youth ministry, a pastor or an adult with whom you serve

- Parent - A parent or guardian

- Other - An employer, coach, teacher or other adult

Reference Applicant's Name: _____

Relationship to Applicant: _____

How long have you known the applicant? _____

The student who has asked you to complete this reference is applying for a student leadership team at the church. As a member of the team they will be challenged emotionally, relationally, and in leadership. They will be called upon to be a role model in all aspects of their life as well as influence other students. Do you believe this applicant is up to the task?

Yes / No

Why?

As a member of the student leadership team, this student will be called upon to attend bi-monthly leadership team meetings as well as attend two leadership training events (possibly overnight). Would you be supportive of this student participating in these events/meetings?

Yes / No

Comments:

On a scale of 1 - 5 with 5 being the highest, how well does the applicant:
- Live a Christian life? 1 2 3 4 5
- Work on a team? 1 2 3 4 5
- Take initiative? 1 2 3 4 5
- Submit to authority? 1 2 3 4 5
- Communicate to others? 1 2 3 4 5
- Listen to others? 1 2 3 4 5
- Lead by example? 1 2 3 4 5
- Encourage a positive attitude? 1 2 3 4 5
- Handle conflict and crisis? 1 2 3 4 5
- Follow through on commitments? 1 2 3 4 5
- Serve others? 1 2 3 4 5

Many students are applying for the 10 positions available on this team. Why should the applicant be chosen for this team?

Student Leader Covenant

Being a student leader is a serious responsibility. It requires being a leader worth following. You cannot expect anyone to respect you as a leader and follow your leadership unless you are willing to live like a leader should. As a part of the responsibility of being a student leader you are asked to agree to each of the statements below:

- ***Relationship with God.*** *I will make my personal relationship with God the number one priority in my life. I will seek to grow by spending time daily with God, finding a spiritual mentor, and surrounding myself with Christians who will challenge me in my faith.*

- ***Godly Lifestyle.*** *As a student leader I understand how I lead my personal life will greatly affect my ability to lead. I will be careful to remain pure in dating relationships and avoid alcohol, tobacco, drugs, and pornography.*

- ***Attend All Leadership Team Meetings:*** *I am committing to attend all Leadership Team meetings. If I have a conflict that is unavoidable I will contact the Team Leader at least one week before the meeting. I understand that if I miss meetings without talking to the Team Leader I may be asked to resign the team.*

- ***Regular Involvement in Youth Group:*** *I understand that as a student leader I need to regularly attend youth group functions.*

- ***Personal Development:*** *I realize that a the Student Leadership Team is focused on developing me as a leader. I commit to doing all the work necessary to becoming a better leader.*

- ***Sacrifice for Others:*** *I understand that I will be asked to sacrifice for others as a leader. I will make that sacrifice willingly.*

- ***Defend the Team:*** *I will never talk bad about any other member of the Leadership Team. I will keep all problems within the confines of the team and commit to working them out.*

- ***Pursuit of Excellence:*** *I am willing to pursue excellence in all I do as a student leader.*

Signed: _____

Date:_____

Introducing/Integrating Leadership Teams into Your Ministry

You have already considered your goals in developing a student leadership program. Now you need to think about what those kids will do within the ministry. How you introduce and integrate your leadership team into your overall student ministry is vital to the long term success of the program. If you neglect this crucial step, it will be easy for students to feel left out. Parents are then likely to misunderstand the goal and volunteers may be unsupportive of the student leaders.

Following are five examples of student leadership teams to give you some ideas. What students can do in youth ministry is only limited by our comfort level and imagination.

Start by considering what role the student leaders will play. Then think through how it will affect the rest of the youth ministry. For example, a great role for student leaders is to plan a major function or event of the youth group. This can work well, but it may also affect your volunteers and other students if the team makes major changes without good communication. Be sure that you examine the ramifications of allowing students to be able to make big changes to the program.

When you are ready to launch your program, emphasize and promote it. Allow your student leaders time in the spotlight. Be sure the rest of the students understand the role of the student leaders as well as the sacrifice they are making. If you have not already done so, consider teaching a series on biblical leadership during the time you kick off the leadership team. Make it a special privilege to be a student leader. Warn your student leaders that their highest calling is serving their fellow leaders. Watch for signs of arrogance in the leaders and address it quickly when you see it. The better job you do of introducing and integrating your leadership program into the fabric of the youth ministry, the fewer problems you will experience along the way.

Designing the Structure for Student Leadership Teams

Now that you have a plan in place you are well on your way. You have overcome the big obstacle of starting your new student leadership team and you have momentum on your side. In this section, we will look at what it takes to develop student leaders, how to maintain a balance in your student leadership program and how to structure your time with your students to be most effective.

Even as things start to get a little easier it is important to stay focused. Many of us often start well but finish poorly. The next obstacle you need to tackle is the structure of your student leadership team: the week-to-week and month-to-month program that you will use to develop your student leaders. Remind yourself of the goal you have for student leaders. Use this goal to focus your efforts in creating a great program of student leadership development. This book contains some great resources to get you started. We have provided 16 sessions (two per month) of great, biblically-based leadership studies to give your team a head start on becoming the leaders that God wants them to be. It is up to you to think about when, where and how often your team will meet. Remember, where you take your team will be up to you.

What projects will the students focus on?

1.

2.

3.

How will you proceed with each project? Note some initial steps below:

How to Develop Student Leaders

At LeaderTreks, our desire is to see transformational change happen in students' lives. We want students to think differently about who they are in Christ. We want them to pursue Him with passion, and we want them to give their lives away for His glory. Based on our experience, students who wholeheartedly pursue leadership development experience transformational change. With this as our goal, we developed a model for how students develop as leaders.

The LeaderTreks Leadership development model is simple:

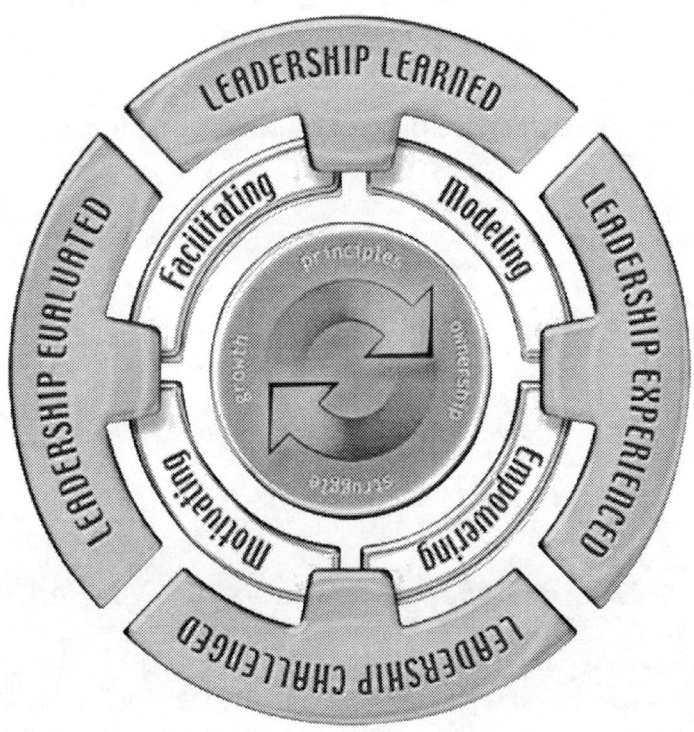

- **Leadership Principles:** Students must learn a set of leadership principles-biblical truths about leadership. The Bible is our foundation for learning about who leaders are and what leaders do.

- **Leadership Experienced**: Students must apply these principles through real leadership experiences. Students need to make decisions that lead to success or failure then live with the consequences of their decisions. It's not enough to talk about leadership-leaders lead.

- **Leadership Challenged:** These experiences have to be challenging; students have to move outside of their comfort zone for transformational change to take place. Too often, we don't challenge students enough and so they remain unchanged and stunted in their spiritual and emotional growth.

- **Leadership Evaluated**: Evaluation is the key that brings the process together. As students learn to ask tough questions, they discover how to apply the leadership lessons to their life. We challenge students to consider how they can do it better next time and how they can make sure they finish strong.

Leadership development is a process; students must have multiple experiences in leadership roles. They must understand the pressures to lead and the humility needed to follow. All of LeaderTreks' services and products are based on this model. Research and experience tell us developing leadership is a continual process. It can be taught. It can be sharpened. However, it doesn't happen by accident.

Lets see how we can apply this practical model for student leadership development to your youth ministry. Consider this simple three-step approach.

1. Teach leadership principles

For students to develop into leaders, they need to know what a leader does. Too often we give students easy tasks like taking attendance and by doing so, think we are teaching leadership. In reality, we are teaching them to be responsible, believing that responsible students make good leaders. Unfortunately, this type of "leader" is not really making any hard decisions or feeling the friction of leadership.

Great student leaders are allowed to think for themselves, determine goals and calculate needed resources. They are able to motivate their peers by casting vision; they navigate obstacles and seek ways to improve.

As mentors, we need to teach leadership principles to students so they can began to understand leadership is about skills and not genetics. Once students understand that they can learn leadership, they will jump at the chance to grow as leaders.

Ask yourself: How well have I communicated leadership principles to my students at this point?

1	2	3	4	5
Very little				Very well

2. Create challenging leadership experiences

Youth workers are often frustrated at developing leaders in their group. They may have spoken on the subject of leadership. Some may have given students the opportunity to lead "ministry teams." However, still little development takes place. What is the problem? The problem is that students don't care about weak leadership roles that don't challenge them. They need a project or mission that engages their hearts. One youth pastor noted the change he saw in his students after they started raising funds for a school in Zambia. The project engaged the hearts of students. They saw the raising of funds as an opportunity to save the weakest of humanity. As they took up this challenge and started to seek ways to meet their goals, they quickly felt the need for greater leadership. These students are now open to learning more about the subject of leadership. As they make decisions and experience success and failure, opportunities exist for teachable moments. Students are then motivated to listen because they are on a mission to save the world. Help your students set a big, scary goal and you will capture their hearts. This is why we use mission trips to develop students into leaders (read more at www.leadertreks.com).

By now, you probably have some leadership projects in mind for your team. Consider the level of challenge of your ideas by ranking them on the Sleep/Stretch scale below. "Sleep" means students could accomplish that goal in their sleep without hardly trying. "Stretch" describes a goal so challenging that it seems next to impossible and will require God's power.

1	2	3	4	5
Sleep				Stretch

3. Be willing to speak truth

We have worked with Campus Crusade to develop trainers in South America to lead LeaderTreks leadership events. They understand the content, but they struggle with knowing when to step in during training and speak hard truth to participants. When you see something that hurts the team taking place, you must be willing to tell others in a direct, loving way that what they are doing is damaging the team. This is tough business. Many people don't have the resolve, but it's the hard work of shaping and molding a leader. This point will make or break your development of student leaders. You will not want to come across as harsh, but you do have to be willing to point out trouble spots so students can identify and overcome them. Fear of what student may think of us or how they will react is a powerful force in keeping us from developing leaders.

If you have a relationship with students based on truth, those students won't "hate you" for lovingly telling them the truth about themselves. They may not like it, but they will respect it. Always follow hard truth with words of encouragement or challenge. Students respond positively when they understand that you care about them. (More articles about developing student leaders can be found in the back of this resource.)

What potential "trouble spots" do you need to address on your team? How will you do so?

Structure for a Meeting

Meeting with student leaders is fun, and sometimes it's the best part of the ministry week. They understand us and we get them. They love our jokes and they want to grow. We could hang out with them forever. The problem is that sometimes we do. When we just hang out with them, the student leadership meeting is more about time with the "good kids" than about learning new leadership principles and skills.

The content of your student leadership meetings matters. Student leadership meetings need to be broken into two parts: part one is Leadership Principles; part two is Leadership Experience. At LeaderTreks, we have discovered that the secret to growing student leaders is to tie principles of leadership to experiences that engage them. Students need to learn and be challenged. By utilizing this two-pronged approach, your student leaders will become more engaged, and your meetings will be more effective.

Part One-LEADERSHIP PRINCIPLES (led by the youth leader)

The first part of the student leader meeting is lead by the youth leader with the goal of teaching leadership principles. Leadership principles such as strategic planning, risk taking or intentional communication are often misunderstood by students but can easily be learned. This time is very important, which is why we have created the Leadership 365 resource. Leadership 365 contains meeting notes and ideas to use in your student leadership program to teach biblical leadership principles. The leader needs to bring these principles to life. Students need to see how the leadership principle intersects with their leadership role.

Part Two-LEADERSHIP EXPERIENCE (led by the students)

The second part of the student leader meeting needs to be lead by students and focused on a leadership experience. Examples of leadership experiences include leadership for mission trips, youth ministry events, small groups and outreach events. When students have real decision-making power in these events, they will be able to put the leadership principles they have learned into practice. Without the opportunity to make decisions that lead to results, students will have no reason to apply the leadership principles. If adults rescue students from poor decisions all they will learn is that adults solve their problems. Let students face the consequences of their decisions. Sometimes failure can be the greatest teacher.

Types of Student Leadership Teams

Gaining an understanding of how to develop student leaders is crucial. The next decision to make is what your student leaders will focus on doing. Student leaders are capable of doing much, but both you and they will be much more successful if you have them focus on a narrow range of ministry options. Below you will find five examples of successful leadership teams. Each of these teams is focused on just one aspect of the youth ministry. As they gain success and experience, students can plan and do more, but it is best to maintain the focus for a specific length of time.

Read the following descriptions for ideas on focused student leadership teams.

Event Leadership Team

Responsibilities: Planning specific events for ministry
Ideal Team Size: 6-10 students
Time Commitment: Seasonal
Level of Leadership Development: Medium

Event Leadership Teams are a type of leadership team that works well for a smaller ministry wanting to start a leadership development program. These teams are effective for smaller youth ministries because they are seasonal. You can have an event team that plans a weekend retreat, outreach bowling night or battle-of-the-sexes night. Commitment to the team is low since they can be seasonal; however the amount of development is also low.

Ministry Leadership Team

Responsibilities: Oversight and Direction of the ministry
Ideal Team Size: 6-10 students
Time Commitment: School Year
Level of Leadership Development: Very High

A Ministry Leadership Team will partner with the youth worker to provide overall leadership to a youth ministry. Students meet with the youth worker on a regular basis and oversee aspects of the ministry. Two students will partner together to oversee various parts of the ministry: welcoming, worship, message planning, events, evangelism, assimilation, website, weekly e-newsletters, etc. Ministry Teams often study leadership during regular meetings. The commitment for this type of team is high, but the return on investment is often very high.

Mission Leadership Team

Responsibilities: Plan, Run, and Participate in a Mission Trip
Ideal Team Size: 10-18 students
Time Commitment: 6 months and 2 weeks on the trip
Level of Leadership Development: Very High

Mission Leadership Teams play a large roll in the planning and executing of annual mission trips. One youth ministry in Dallas has found that this is one of the most effective uses of student leaders. Students begin to buy into the mission and commit their hearts and time to seeing the place they will serve reached for Christ. LeaderTreks has a program specifically designed to use trips to develop student leaders and has seen the positive impact they have had for more than 12 years.

Global Leadership Team

Responsibilities: Identify an international mission and educate and motivate others to give
Ideal Team Size: 8-12 students
Time Commitment: Variable
Level of Leadership Development: Very High

Global Leadership Teams identify, advocate and raise funds for a charitable project. Global Teams can raise money for AIDS, water systems, orphanages, international schools and numerous other charities. The team will find ways to raise awareness among in the youth ministry attendees as well as the church and even school. One Global Team in Illinois this year raised more than $125,000 for a hospital in Zambia and hosted a local AIDS conference for high school students. The key to making this work is to help the students identify a project that piques their interest and excitement.

Small Group Leader Team

Responsibilities: Lead a Small Group
Ideal Team Size: 2 Students per Small Group
Time Commitment: School Year
Level of Leadership Development: High Discipleship, Medium Leadership

The primary reason that small groups fail is that their leader is under equipped; therefore, this type of leadership team should be used with extreme caution. When students are not first taught how to teach, they will not feel comfortable. They will not enjoy it, and they will often give up quickly. The Small Group Leader Team can be very effective when adult volunteers aren't available. High school students can be asked to lead small groups for middle school students, for example.

Which of these teams most suits your current students? Which teams tap into your passions/talents?

As you decide the focus of your leadership team, be sure to be realistic about what can happen within your ministry context. Talk it over with your adults and make an informed decision. Although each team has its own unique characteristics, all are effective opportunities.

Student Leadership During a Ministry Year (Calendar)

It is best to lay out a calendar for your entire leadership program in advance. That way the duration and responsibilities of the team will be clear before you even start. For some ministries, it would make the most sense to plan your leadership calendar around the school year. In this situation, you would choose student leaders in the fall and meet with them during the fall and spring semesters. For leadership teams that are shorter term in length, you may only meet for a few weeks or months. Determining your calendar ahead of time will make the process much easier.

When you make your calendar, you will need to balance the development of the students with the leadership role the students will play. Spend about half your time teaching and discipling them as growing leaders. Use the resources in this book as a platform to teach your students biblical principles on leadership. Also consider using retreats as opportunities to grow your students in powerful ways. At LeaderTreks, we provide leadership retreats where our staff teach you and your students how to be more effective leaders. Check out www.leadertreks.com for more information. Use the other half of your time together to plan and execute the leadership responsibilities of the team.

Special events are bolded in the following sample calendar. Brainstorm what events you would like to do with your student leadership team.

Here is a sample leadership calendar for a school year:

Week 1: Announce student leaders to youth group.

Have first Student Leadership Team Meeting (1-1 1/2 hours)

Week 2: 10-minute quick check-in at youth group

Week 3: Student Leadership Team Meeting

Week 4: Student Leadership Retreat (Foundations of Leadership)

Week 5: Student Leadership Team Meeting

Week 6: 10-minute quick check-in at youth group

Week 7: Student Leadership Team Meeting

Week 8: 10-minute quick check-in at youth group

Week 9: Student Leadership Team Meeting

Week 10: 1st Student-led outreach event

Week 11: Student Leadership Team Meeting

Week 12 -14: Holiday Break

Week 15: Student Leadership Team Meeting

Week 16: 10-minute quick check-in at youth group

Week 17: Student Leadership Team Meeting

Week 18: 10-minute quick check-in at youth group

Week 19: Student Leadership Team Meeting

Week 20: 10-minute quick check-in at youth group

Week 21: Student Leadership Team Meeting

Week 22: 2nd Student-led outreach event

Week 23: Student Leadership Team Meeting

Week 24: Student-led mission trip

Adult Roles in Student Leadership

Communicating about Student Leadership to Parents, Church Leaders and Adult Volunteers

Many student leadership teams fail because the youth worker has not done the hard work of sharing a compelling vision for developing leadership within the youth group. It is vital for the success of your leadership team to include everyone who has a stake in your youth ministry. When starting a student leadership program it will be natural for many people in the church to have questions. It is easy to overlook three very important groups of people: church leadership, parents and adult volunteers.

- Church leaders will want to know your intentions-in other words, how far you are going to carry student decision-making.

- Parents will want to know who is going to be on the team and what the criteria is for choosing student leaders.

- The adult volunteers in the ministry will want to know what their role is in a student-leader program.

These are all good questions. For you to have a successful program, you need to deal with them honesty and openly.

Church leaders - We have found that the church leadership will often believe in a student-leader program. After all, who can better understand the need for growing new leaders than those charged with leading their own congregations? They will, however, be cautious of students making big decisions on their own. Remember, part of their job is to minimize risk. Let's face it-the idea of students being in charge doesn't exactly scream "risk free." When you say "students will be in charge" the adults are envisioning a food fight followed by a small urban riot. When presenting the program to the church leadership, fully explain the scope of the program. Detail what decisions students will be making. Describe the boundaries you intend to put in place to ensure safety. Also, clearly explain how the program is based on a mentoring relationship with an adult. Be clear and complete when making your presentation. By having your church leadership on board you will ensure support even if the program experiences difficult times.

Who in church leadership will need to know about your plans (pastor, staff, etc.)? How will you communicate with them? When? What was their response?

Parents - Parental support for the leadership team is essential, and nothing could be worse if they feel left out of the process. Parents will want to know two things: 1) Who is on the team? and 2) What is the criteria for getting on the team? Be consistent and honest when you answer. It is easy to feel as if you need to tell parents what they want to hear. Resist this temptation and be honest. If their son or daughter doesn't meet the criteria for being on the team, encourage the parents by explaining the conditions they need to meet. Also remember to be consistent; if you let a student on the team that doesn't meet the criteria and you keep others off, nothing will ruin your credibility faster. The ramifications could be bigger than you think.

Consider this plan. Call a parent meeting to explain the reasons for having a student leadership team, the structure of the program and how students will be selected. Before the meeting, ask a few parents to serve with you and your volunteer team on a committee that selects the student leaders. This will give you the benefit of support by not making all the decisions alone. This also gives ownership to the parents by being involved in the process. Announce who is on the committee so all the parents understand. Communicate well and often! Let parents know the deadlines for getting applications into your office. Inform them when the team will be announced, and let them know how you will tell the students who are not selected. (It is best to have a personal meeting with students that don't make the team to let them know why they didn't qualify and what they can do to increase their chances next year.)

What parental pitfalls have you encountered and/or avoided so far in the process of starting your program?

Adult Volunteers - Surprisingly, adult volunteers often struggle with student leadership teams. This is because they are afraid to lose their roles or positions to the students. As the youth director, everybody knows your role. However, the adult volunteers might not feel as secure in their role. You know the decisions and responsibilities that you want to turn over to the student leaders, but your volunteers may not see it the same way. Adult leaders often don't buy-in for reasons like these.

The answer is to retrain your adults-move them from chaperones to mentors. Realistically, you don't need van drivers and cooks; you need adults who will pour their lives into the lives of students no matter how messy it gets. By helping your volunteers see that their role is to develop deep relationship with students, you will give them a vision for the future and their ministry that is powerful and inspiring.

Present your ideas about a student leadership team soon after getting church approval and before going to parents. Volunteers will help answer parents' questions and help identify potential student leaders. Help them understand changes they will have to make early on in the process in order to ensure a smooth transition to the new program. Be sure that you help them understand how they can help develop student leaders through mentoring relationships.

What initial resistance have you met so far from your adult leaders? How have you responded?

The key to helping these different groups of people is to communicate. Don't just share the reasons behind the program once; state it over and over again until people are able to repeat your intentions back to you in a way that lets you know they "get it." Starting a student leadership team sounds great, but remember to be intentional if you want to get the church leaders, parents and adult volunteers on your side. It will make all the difference.

Section Three:
The Character and Heart of Leaders

Semester One

A well-prepared leader leads from the heart. The actions of a leader are based on the belief that "doing" leadership always flows from first "being" a leader that people want to follow.

Lesson 1

Why Study Leadership?

Introduction:

Godly leadership changes people and organizations for the better. It's how God empowers His people to accomplish His goals. The local church is just now awakening to the importance of training people to be leaders in God's Kingdom. Do you consider leadership training to be of equal importance in a student ministry curriculum as other aspects of discipleship training? Talk with your students about this important question. Decide together how you will prioritize leadership in your student ministry.

In this lesson, students will:

- Decide how to make leadership training a priority for God's people

- Examine five reasons why leadership is important

- Study Nehemiah's leadership example

Going Public:

Do you think an emphasis on student leadership training is as important as other aspects of discipleship? Why or why not?

Note: You're looking for the most honest answer possible. Challenge students to "go public" with their fears and emotions as they relay their own personal experiences.

Expert Opinions:

"On the surface, the answer to why leadership is important to society is simple - without leadership there would be chaos." *Robert Burke*

"Leadership is important because it's all about direction. True leaders help us move forward, as a person, as a community, as a nation." *Dan Kahl*

"Leadership is vital for healthy churches. Leadership is vital for the church to influence the society in which we live. Leadership is vital to encourage church growth. Leadership is vital to enable Christians to grow in ministry. Leadership is vital!" *The Teal Trust*

"As the leaders go, so goes the church." *Elmer L. Towns*

"If anyone wants to provide leadership in the church, good!" *1 Timothy 3:1 (The Message)*

Getting Focused:

To introduce this lesson, read the following story to students about Ernest Shackleton's dangerous expedition to Antarctica.

The following ad ran in a London newspaper in 1913:

Men Wanted for Hazardous Journey

Small wages. Bitter cold. Long months of complete darkness. Constant danger. Safe return doubtful. Honour and recognition in case of success. - Ernest Shackleton.

In late 1914, Shackleton set sail for the Antarctic with a 28-man crew, many of whom had responded to this ad. His goal was to cross the entire Antarctic continent, in his mind the last great polar challenge. Only three days after leaving shore, the wooden ship Endurance met with floating chunks of ice and massive icebergs. Eventually the ice crushed the hull. The crew scrambled off the ship onto an ice floe. For the next five months, Shackleton kept the crew busy working on tasks, all the while living off of rationed food. Two unsuccessful attempts were made to haul the lifeboats to open water and soon they discovered the ice floe had begun to melt. This time, everyone scurried into the lifeboats and spent the next seven days shivering at sea. Shackleton stoically stood with tiller in hand (a long stick attached to the rutter) in an attempt to rally the crew's morale, even though he knew there was no hope of rescue.

Finally, he made a desperate decision when they reached deserted Elephant Island. He and five others left the island and sailed to the nearest whaling station at South Georgia Island-17 days across 800 miles through massive waves, powerful winds and even a hurricane using only primitive navigation instruments.

They made it to the island, but were devastated when they found that the whaling station was on the opposite side of the island. Tired, thirsty, hungry, frostbitten and their lifeboat destroyed, Shackleton's team traversed treacherous glaciers and steep mountains to reach help after a 36-hour journey. In a borrowed boat, Shackleton's team sailed back to Elephant Island unsure of what awaited them. As they approached the shore, Shackleton counted the figures in the distance. Amazingly, everyone survived the ordeal. A friend summed it up best. "When disaster strikes and all hope is gone, get down on your knees and pray for Shackleton."

Ask:
How would you respond to this ad?
Robert Burke once claimed that there would be chaos without leadership. Why would there be chaos during this expedition across the Antarctic without leadership?
How did Shackleton display leadership? Try to list as many examples as possible.

Possible answers include:

1. Kept crew busy
2. Rationed food
3. Attempted to reach safety
4. Encouraged morale by standing at the tiller
5. Reached dry land (Elephant Island/South Georgia Island)
6. Led rescue party
7. Demonstrated courage
8. Endured same hardships as followers

Say something like:
It is important for us to study leadership because it has the potential to change people, organizations and impossible situations for the better. Does God care about leadership? Is it important for students to be leaders? The Bible seems to say so because it teaches us important lessons about what leaders do and what they are like. Leadership influences the society in which we live and the destinies of those around us. Without strong leaders influencing our lives, we would not become who we are meant to be, nor achieve what we are meant to achieve. Let's look at five specific reasons why leadership is important:

1. **First, leadership is important because it causes change.** God uses leaders to change the world by changing the status quo.

   Ask:
   Are you satisfied with the "status quo" among your peers? In your school? In your church? In your world?

2. **Second, leadership is important because it gives people a common purpose.** People want to live for something greater than themselves. Leadership makes our biggest dreams possible when we work together to achieve it.

   Ask:
   When was a time you worked as a team to achieve something you could not do by yourself? What did you learn?

3. **Third, leadership is important because it provides organization.** Without leadership, there would be chaos. Social structures would not budge, countries would have weak political systems, schools would be ineffective and the church would never have grown past the original twelve disciples.

   Ask:
   Someone has said, "Everything hinges on leadership." Do you agree or disagree? Explain.

4. **Fourth, leadership is important because it enables people to realize their potential**. Leadership challenges us to grow and mature. It forces us to see a vision of who we are in Christ.

   Ask:
   Do you feel that you have reached all of your potential in Christ? Why or why not?

5. **Fifth, leadership is important because it enhances productivity.** The biggest leadership challenge is to persuade people to work together who don't necessarily want to cooperate.

   Ask:
   What do you think of the following acronym for team: "Together Everyone Accomplishes More"?

Say something like:
It's interesting to note that the Bible uses personal examples to teach us successful principles of leadership. Instead of reading specific leadership principles, the Bible gives us a story about someone in leadership-and challenges us to learn from his or her life. The following glimpse into Nehemiah's leadership is one such example.

Growing Deeper:
Nehemiah was in charge of rebuilding the wall around the city of Jerusalem. Although they worked in the midst of their enemies, the city was vulnerable to attack and virtually defenseless without the wall. He organized the people into groups and assigned them to specific sections of the wall, including several areas identified as "gates."

Read the following passage from Nehemiah 3:14-16 and identify principles, practices and personal qualities that made Nehemiah an effective leader:

14 The Dung Gate was repaired by Malkijah son of Recab, ruler of the district of Beth Hakkerem. He rebuilt it and put its doors and bolts and bars in place. 15 The Fountain Gate was repaired by Shallun son of Col-Hozeh, ruler of the district of Mizpah. He rebuilt it, roofing it over and putting its doors and bolts and bars in place. He also repaired the wall of the Pool of Siloam, by the King's Garden, as far as the steps going down from the City of David. 16 Beyond him, Nehemiah son of Azbuk, ruler of a half-district of Beth Zur, made repairs up to a point opposite the tombs of David, as far as the artificial pool and the House of the Heroes.

Ask:
We know Nehemiah wrote this book in first-person and he was intimately acquainted with the people and every detail of their work. What does this teach you about his leadership?
Why did he spend so much time on noting "who was where"?
Why was it important for Nehemiah to assign a section to himself?
Why was this task a God-sized challenge for Nehemiah?

Help students summarize their answers in the following possible themes about Nehemiah's leadership:

1. Leaders **involve people** from every walk of life.
2. Leaders **know** the people they lead.
3. Leaders **set the example**.
4. Leaders take on **tough assignments**.

"Explorers" Case Study Activity

In this activity, students will analyze a situation and use their leadership skills to determine the best outcome.

Instructions

Divide students into two teams. Pass out a copy of the chart below to each team. Explain that they will consider a case study of two leaders who raced to be the first to reach the South Pole in 1911. The chart gives the details of Expedition A, led by English explorer Robert Scott and Expedition B, led by Norwegian explorer Raold Amundsen. Instruct students to review the chart. Each team must unanimously choose which expedition to join and explain why.

After students have explained which expedition they would choose, debrief with the following information:

In Scott's expedition, all of the men died. Amundsen, however, was successful. Some of the keys to his success include:

1. Experience: Amundsen spent two years preparing for this expedition.
2. Mission: He focused on one goal.
3. Motive: His mission was his motive instead of the media circus that surrounded Scott.
4. Staff: His team was small and professional.
5. Team Skills: He developed the specific skills needed to succeed.
6. Transport: He relied on simple modes of transportation.
7. Equipment: Custom-made and cutting edge. Their clothing, for example, was one piece and kept their head warmer; animal skins trapped body heat.

Factor	Expedition A	Expedition B
LEADER'S EXPERIENCE	41 years old 19 year naval career Promoted to lieutenant 3 years Antarctic experience	39 years old Former medical student Licensed ship captain 5 years in Arctic & Antarctic
MISSION	1) To reach the South Pole 2) To conduct scientific experiments	To reach the South Pole
MOTIVE	To advance naval career	To be the first to the South Pole
PLANNING	Six months Extensive research Focused on scientific research	Two years Hands-on field experience Systematic study of every detail
STAFF SELECTIONS	72 men, 33 dogs, 3 sleds;19 ponies Large, diverse group Many academics and navy men Professional scientists Amateur polar travelers	19 men, 100 dogs; 4 sleds Small, mobile group Olympic skier; 4 navigators World-class dog driver Professional polar travelers
TEAM SKILLS	Diverse skills (naval, academic, scientific, and medical)	Dog sledding; Survival skills;
PRE-TRIP MEDIA	Under intense media scrutiny Departed with great fanfare	Kept plans secret Departed without any fanfare
TRANSPORT TO THE ANTARCTIC	Whaling ship Heavily loaded, 33 dogs (from Siberia) Motorized sleds Ponies pulled sleds Men pulled sleds (man-hauling)	Schooner Diesel engine Handled by crew of 6 100 Dogs (from Greenland) Dogs pulled lightweight sleds Men pulled on skis behind sled
EQUIPMENT	Purchased "over the counter" One innovation: motorized sleds	Custom-made Many innovations (lightweight sleds with easy access to supplies, and tents with floors)
CLOTHING	2-piece: canvas, separate hats	1-piece: animal skins and fur
PREPARATIONS IN THE ANTARCTIC	Arrived first Camped 87 miles further north Established 2 supply depots Separate officer/crew quarters Conducted required classes 3 trial runs to test man-hauling	Arrived 70 days later Camped 87 miles further south Established 7 supply depots Each man cared for 14-15 dogs Competitions with prizes Daily work schedule
ROUTE / TEAM	Same route as earlier attempt Left 5 days after Expedition B 12 explorers (6 for support) 6 constituted polar team	New route, never used before Left first for South Pole 5 explorers Same 5 constituted polar team
DECISIONS	Rigid adherence to naval discipline and chain of command	Open to ideas & delegated responsibility for decisions

Ask students:
Did you choose the right expedition? Why or why not?
The two team's decision-making ability differed (see chart). How do you think this affected the outcome?
In what way is leadership in the church a matter of life or death, spiritually speaking?

Close this lesson by praying for team focus as you begin this "expedition" into the heart of leadership. Call students by name and pray for each one to hear from God over the coming weeks and months regarding His plans and purposes.

Lesson Summary:

Leadership is important because:

- It causes change.

- It gives a common purpose.

- It provides organization.

- It enables people to realize their potential.

- It enhances productivity.

From The Student Guide

Lesson One

Why Study Leadership?

Introduction:
Godly leadership changes people and organizations for the better. It's how God empowers His people to accomplish His goals.

Going Public:
Do you think an emphasis on student leadership training is as important as other aspects of discipleship? Why or why not?

Getting Focused:
Leadership is important because:

1.

2.

3.

4.

5.

Growing Deeper:
Nehemiah 3:14-16

Nehemiah's leadership shows us:

1. Leaders _____ from every walk of life.

2. Leaders _____ the people they lead.

3. Leaders _____.

4. Leaders take on _____.

13

Lesson Summary:
Leadership is important because:

- It causes _____.

- It gives a _____ purpose.

- It provides _____.

- It enables people to realize their _____.

- It _____ _____.

14

Lesson 2

Leadership Can Be Learned

Introduction

Have you ever heard that someone is a "born leader"? That may be a popular figure of speech, but it's not true. Leadership can be learned. Unfortunately, many students are under the false assumption that leaders are born, not made. In fact, a major study by George Barna once found that while 85% of business leaders believe that leadership can be learned, 85% of students believe that individuals are born leaders.

In this lesson, students will:

- Understand leadership can be learned and that leaders are made, not born.

- Learn the formula for transformational leadership.

- Consider the leadership development of Joshua.

Going Public:

Do you think God really intends for you to be a leader? Why or why not?

Note: You're looking for the most honest answer possible. Challenge students to "go public" with their fears and emotions as they relay their own personal experiences.

Expert Opinions:

"Leadership cannot really be taught. It can only be learned." *Harold Geneen*

"Good leaders develop through a never-ending process of self-study, education, training, and experience." *Manual on military leadership*

"Leaders aren't born they are made. And they are made just like anything else, through hard work. And that's the price we'll have to pay to achieve that goal, or any goal." *Vince Lombardi*

"The most dangerous leadership myth is that leaders are born -- that there is a genetic factor to leadership. This myth asserts that people simply either have certain charismatic qualities or not. That's nonsense; in fact, the opposite is true. Leaders are made rather than born." *Warren G. Bennis*

"Let the wonderful kindness and the understanding that come from our Lord and Savior Jesus Christ help you to keep on growing. Praise Jesus now and forever! Amen." *2 Peter 3:18 (CEV)*

Getting Focused:
To introduce this lesson to students, say something like:

Let's take a poll. How many of you believe leaders are born, not made? (count hands).

A major study by George Barna once found that while 85% of business leaders believe that leadership can be learned, 85% of students believe that you are born a leader. Leadership is not something some students are born with and others aren't. There is no leadership gene that some students have and others don't. Being a leader is not genetic or hereditary. It is a set of skills that can be learned and developed.

Focus on the quote below by having a student read it aloud:

"The most dangerous leadership myth is that leaders are born-that there is a genetic factor to leadership. This myth asserts that people simply either have certain charismatic qualities or not. That's nonsense; in fact, the opposite is true. Leaders are made rather than born."   Warren G. Bennis, author and leadership expert

Ask:
Why is it dangerous to believe leaders are born, not made?

Possible answers may include:

- If so, only a few people can be leaders
- It could be an excuse not to lead
- It focuses on personality rather than character
- Makes leadership seem rare and unattainable

Say something like:
You know more about leadership than you think you know. Throughout your life, you have assimilated bits of knowledge about this topic, organized the information internally and stored it in your mind for later use. God designed our intellect to work this way without us even being aware of the process. When we combine our resources, we will discover that we have a large pool of information on the subject.

Ask:
What do you want to learn about leadership that you don't already know?

"Know It All" Activity
This activity challenges students to compile information about leadership that they already know while stimulating a desire to learn more.

Equipment:

Large piece of paper
Copies of chart for each student
Pens

Instructions:

Provide copies of the following chart. Explain to students that the chart asks them to list what they know about leadership in three columns: "What we know," "What we want to know," and "How we can find the answers." In three minutes, students should complete at least two entries in each of these three columns. For now, leave the fourth column blank labeled, "What we learned."

What we Know about Leadership	What we Want to know about Leadership	How we can find the answer about Leadership	What we Learned about Leadership

As students prepare their charts, draw the chart on a large piece of paper. After the time is up, select one student to record the group's answers.

Ask:
What is one item you listed in the first column?" Limit the list to a total of five entries. Then complete the second and third columns in the same manner.
How many of you learned something you didn't know about leadership by someone else's answers?

Say something like:
We know a great deal about leadership, but the combination of everyone's knowledge is always greater than what we can know alone. Obviously, there is a lot to learn about leadership. Fortunately, leadership is a set of skills that can be taught and can be learned. Anyone at anytime can exercise leadership if the proper principles are applied.

Tell students to write down the following formula near their charts:

Leadership Principles + Leadership Experience = Transformational Leadership

There is a set of leadership principles that, when applied, allow normal people to do extraordinary things. Some of these principles include communication, problem solving, focus, risk taking, conflict resolution and navigating obstacles. A great place to start in leadership is to learn how to use these principles effectively.

It is not enough, however, to learn principles of leadership. Knowledge by itself doesn't make a person an effective leader. Practical experience is where leadership principles come to life. You learn to be a leader by leading. Leadership development occurs when you apply leadership principles to specific situations.

This process is summarized this way:

Leadership Principles + Leadership Experience = Transformational Leadership

Transformational leadership takes place when the leaders experience what they know about leadership. Their influence brings positive and needed change to individuals and organizations. It is a powerful and effective leadership approach everyone can learn.

Growing Deeper:

Read the following passage from Exodus 24:12-18. The Israelites have escaped from Egypt and are looking for leadership to know what to do next. Look for leadership principles that Joshua (Moses' aide and eventual successor) likely learned from Moses during this specific experience with God.

12 The LORD said to Moses, "Come up to me on the mountain and stay here, and I will give you the tablets of stone, with the law and commands I have written for their instruction." 13 Then Moses set out with Joshua his aide, and Moses went up on the mountain of God. 14 He said to the elders, "Wait here for us until we come back to you. Aaron and Hur are with you, and anyone involved in a dispute can go to them. When Moses went up on the mountain, the cloud covered it, 16 and the glory of the LORD settled on Mount Sinai. For six days the cloud covered the mountain, and on the seventh day the LORD called to Moses from within the cloud. 17 To the Israelites the glory of the LORD looked like a consuming fire on top of the mountain. 18 Then Moses entered the cloud as he went on up the mountain. And he stayed on the mountain forty days and forty nights."

Possible answers could include:

1. Moses left instructions on what to do in his absence
2. Moses obeyed God and did what he said. Joshua followed his example.
2. Joshua witnessed God's work because Moses brought him along.
3. Joshua experienced what Moses experienced-Moses did not just tell him about it later.

Say something like:
Joshua was not born a leader. Moses taught Joshua about leadership through personal experience. During your lifetime you have learned to do many things. Leadership may not have been one of them. You can watch someone's example, but you must be willing to also learn specific principles.

Ask:
Are you open to learning more about leadership than you know now?
Are you open to experiencing leadership on a new level?

Go back to the chart students used earlier in the lesson. Complete the fourth column about what they learned about leadership based on today's lesson. Close in prayer, asking God to help these principles begin to influence students' perspective on leadership.

Lesson Summary:

- Leadership can be **learned**.

- The place to start is to learn key leadership **principles**.

- Leadership principles **come alive** through leadership experience.

- Leadership Principles + Leadership Experience = **Transformational Leadership**

Lesson Two

Leadership Can Be Learned

Introduction:
Leadership can be learned. Unfortunately, many students are under the false assumption that leaders are born, not made.

Going Public:
Do you think God really intends for you to be a leader? Why or why not?

Getting Focused:
"The most dangerous leadership myth is that leaders are born -- that there is a genetic factor to leadership. This myth asserts that people simply either have certain charismatic qualities or not. That's nonsense; in fact, the opposite is true. Leaders are made rather than born." Warren G. Bennis

What we Know about Leadership	What we Want to know about Leadership	How we can find the answer about Leadership	What we Learned about Leadership

15

Growing Deeper:
- Exodus 24:12-18
- Joshua learned about leadership by personal experience with Moses.

Lesson Summary:
- Leadership can be _____.
- The place to start is to learn key leadership _____.
- Leadership principles _____ through leadership experience.
- Leadership Principles + Leadership Experience = _____ _____

16

Lesson Three

Leadership Involves Being and Doing

Introduction:
There are two sides to leadership: doing and being. The doing side is how leaders act; the being side is who leaders are. The doing side relates to the leader's conduct and actions; the being side refers to the leader's character and attitudes.

In this lesson, students will:
- Realize that there are two sides to leadership-doing and being.
- Understand that each side is needed to be an effective leader.
- Study an example in Mary's life on "being" with Jesus.
- Realize that being a godly leader is foundational to knowing how to act like one.

Going Public:
Which is easier; to be a Christian or just to act like one?

Note: You're looking for the most honest answer possible. Challenge students to "go public" with their fears and emotions as they relay their own personal experiences.

Epert Opinions:
"Follow effective action with quiet reflection. From the quiet reflection will come even more effective action." *Peter Drucker*

"We can teach leadership doing. But we can't teach leadership being. That's an inside job. It's an unending journey of personal discovery and learning." *Jim Clemmer*

"We are so obsessed with doing that we have no time and no imagination left for being. As a result, men are valued not for what they are but for what they do or what they have-for their usefulness." *Thomas Merton*

"Ministry is not primarily what God is doing through me, it is what God is doing in me." *Unknown*

"Very early in the morning, while it was still dark, Jesus got up, left the house and went off to a solitary place, where he prayed." *Mark 1:35*

Getting Focused:
To introduce this lesson, say something like:

There are two sides to leadership: doing and being. The doing side is how leaders act; the being side is who leaders are. The doing side relates to the leader's conduct and actions; the being side refers to the leader's character and attitudes. Both are essential to leadership-you can't have one without the other.

Doing:*
Leadership involves doing. A true leader is defined by action. Actions truly do speak louder than words. When the chance comes to stand for the truth no matter the cost, it is the true leader who is the first to rise to the challenge.

Note that the second semester of Leadership 365 focuses on the "doing" side of leadership, while the first semester establishes a foundation of godly character-"being" a leader.

Say something like:
Together we will create a list for the "doing" side of leadership. These are the skills, abilities and actions that a leader uses to influence people and equip a team for success. For example, leaders must have the ability to set goals. Someone has said, "If you don't know where you're going, any road will get you there."

Write "DOING" and "BEING" at the top of 2 columns on a large piece of paper where everyone can see it. Ask for a volunteer to serve as discussion recorder.

Ask:
What skills, abilities and actions do leaders need to influence people and equip teams?

Potential answers to write under the column "DOING" include:

- Focus
- Vision
- Risk Taking
- Goal Setting
- Problem Solving
- Communication
- Conflict Resolution
- Modeling leadership for others

Being:
Leadership also involves being. True leaders are defined by their character. In fact, what you do as a leader always flows out of who you are. That is why we are going to spend this semester focusing first on the character of a leader, then the tasks of a leader.

Say something like:
Together we will create a list for the "being" side of leadership. These are all the character qualities and personal attributes that leaders must possess if they are going to influence people and equip a team to reach their goals. For example, leaders must be people of integrity. Someone has said that the person you are when no one is looking is who you really are.

Refer to the second column, "BEING."

Ask:
What character qualities or attributes do leaders need to influence people and equip teams?

Potential answers to write under the column "BEING" include:

- Humility

- Commitment

- Integrity

- Faith

- Obedience

- Courage

- Wisdom

- Compassion

- Perseverance

- Vision

"Character Continuum" Activity

If leadership involves being, then we should take time to examine our character. Students will accomplish this goal by using a self-evaluation exercise.

Instructions

Provide the student sheet with the following continuum.

Listed below are five principles for developing the area of "being." After reading each principle, tell students to evaluate the current status of their life by marking an "X" on the line. Encourage students to pray for guidance before they begin the self-evaluation.

1. Living out of Quiet

We tend to be so busy that we can't even hear Christ's voice amidst the hustle and bustle of daily life. We must carve out time each day to get alone with Christ, worship Him in our hearts, read His Word, pray for the needs of others and ourselves and listen to His still, small voice.

In this area I am ...

_____

Weak   Growing   Strong

2. Doing out of Being

The world's mindset is so deeply ingrained in us that we try to please God through our spiritual achievements. We equate performance with God's blessing. But God is far more concerned with our character than our accomplishments. His greatest desire is for us to be transformed into the image of His Son. He wants to mold and shape us so that our conduct flows out of our character.

In this area I am ...

_____
Weak   Growing   Strong

3. Surrendering out of Trusting

Christians tend to keep God in the bullpen until we need Him to enter the game. We trust our own abilities, strength and power. When a situation arises that we can't handle, we call on God to help us. But God wants us to trust His presence, power and provision moment by moment. He longs for us to surrender our lives to Him completely and irrevocably. By trusting Him we become strong when we are weak.

In this area I am ...

_____
Weak   Growing   Strong

4. Leading out of Listening

God speaks to us throughout our day through His creation, His Word, other people, our consciences and His Spirit. The adventure of the Christian life is to hear God prompting us to do something on His behalf and to obey Him without delay. Jesus said that His sheep know His voice and follow Him. In this area I am ...

_____
Weak   Growing   Strong

5. Growing out of Pruning

Gods wants us to live fruitful lives. As a gardener prunes vines to make them more fruitful, God prunes our lives according to our needs. If there is sin in our lives, He progressively disciplines us through rebuking, chastening and scourging until we confess and repent. If we are walking with God, He will mold and shape our character through various trials so we become more Christ-centered and less self-centered. He wants us to learn from these experiences so we don't have to repeat them.

In this area I am ...

_____
Weak   Growing   Strong

Ask:
Which principle listed above do you need to focus on this week?
What do you need to do to become stronger in this area?

Growing Deeper:

Read the following passage in Luke 10:38-41. Write down the leadership principles related to "being" that are reflected in the life of Mary.

39She had a sister called Mary, who sat at the Lord's feet listening to what he said. 40But Martha was distracted by all the preparations that had to be made. 41"Martha, Martha," the Lord answered, "you are worried and upset about many things, 42but only one thing is needed. Mary has chosen what is better, and it will not be taken away from her."

Ask:
Which character in the story do you relate to most?
Why do you think that Mary make her choice?
Who demonstrated greater leadership ability, Mary or Martha? Why?

Listed below are suggested principles related to "being":

- Mary spent time with Jesus.

- Mary listened to what Jesus said.

- Her relationship with Jesus was Mary's priority.

Lesson Summary:

- There are two sides to leadership—**doing and being**.

- Each side is needed to be an **effective** leader.

- "Being" a godly leader is **foundational** to knowing how to act like one.

From The Student Guide

Lesson Three

Leadership Involves Doing and Being

Introduction:
The doing side of leadership relates to the leader's conduct and actions; the being side refers to the leader's character and attitudes.

Going Public:
Which is easier; to be a Christian or just to act like one?

Getting Focused:

1. Living out of Quiet

We tend to be so busy that we can't even hear Christ's voice amidst the hustle and bustle of daily life. We must carve out time each day to get alone with Christ, worship Him in our hearts, read His Word, pray for the needs of others and ourselves and listen to His still, small voice.

In this area I am ...

Weak	Growing	Strong

2. Doing out of Being

The world's mindset is so deeply ingrained in us that we try to please God through our spiritual achievements. We equate performance with God's blessing. But God is far more concerned with our character than our accomplishments. His greatest desire is for us to be transformed into the image of His Son. He wants to mold and shape us so that our conduct flows out of our character.

In this area I am ...

Weak	Growing	Strong

17

3. Surrendering out of Trusting

Christians tend to keep God in the bullpen until we need Him to enter the game. We trust in our own abilities, strength and power. When a situation arises that we can't handle, we call on God to help us. But God wants us to trust His presence, power and provision moment by moment. He longs for us to surrender our lives to Him completely and irrevocably. By trusting Him we become strong when we are weak.

In this area I am ...

Weak	Growing	Strong

4. Leading out of Listening

God speaks to us throughout our day through His creation, His Word, other people, our consciences, and His Spirit. Part of the adventure of the Christian life is to hear God prompting us to do something on His behalf and to obey Him without delay. Jesus said that His sheep know His voice and follow Him. In this area I am ...

Weak	Growing	Strong

5. Growing out of Pruning

Gods wants us to live fruitful lives. As a gardener prunes vines to make them more fruitful, God prunes our lives according to our needs. If there is sin in our lives, He progressively disciplines us through rebuking, chastening, and scourging until we confess and repent. If we are walking with God, He will mold and shape our character through various trials so we become more Christ-centered and less self-centered. He wants us to learn from these experiences so we don't have to repeat them.

In this area I am ...

Weak	Growing	Strong

18

Leadership**365**

Growing Deeper:
Read Luke 10:38-41. Mary prioritized "being" over "doing."

Lesson Summary:
- Realize that there are two sides to leadership-_____.
- Each side is needed to be an _____ leader.
- "Being" a godly leader is _____ to knowing how to act like one.

19

Lesson Four

Leaders Are Humble

Introduction:
Humility is having a modest view of one's own worth; it is a key quality of leaders.

In this lesson, students will:
- Identify a key character quality of all true heroes.
- Study the example of Jesus in the area of humility.
- Take a survey asking people to identify their hero and why. (optional)

Going Public:
How comfortable would you be with someone calling you a "hero"?

Note: You're looking for the most honest answer possible. Challenge students to "go public" with their fears and emotions as they relay their own personal experiences.

Expert Opinions:
"Humility is like underwear, essential, but indecent if it shows" *Helen Nielsen*

"What makes humility so desirable is the marvelous thing it does to us; it creates in us a capacity for the closest possible intimacy with God" *Monica Baldwin*

"Humility does not mean thinking less of yourself than of other people, nor does it mean having a low opinion of your own gifts. It means freedom from thinking about yourself at all." *William Temple*

"Be humble or you'll stumble." *Dwight L. Moody*

"But he gives us more grace. That is why Scripture says: 'God opposes the proud but gives grace to the humble.'" *James 4:6*

Getting Focused:
To introduce this lesson, pair students and give them four minutes to answer this question: "Who is your hero and why?"

Who are the heroes of today? A nationwide survey conducted in 2003 by the Barron Prize found that:

"Only half of American teens have a hero."

"Of those teens who did name a well-known hero, more than half named a movie star, musician or athlete."

"More than twice as many teens cited as their heroes Superman and Spiderman than cited Abraham Lincoln, Gandhi or Martin Luther King, Jr."

"Apart from family members, only three women were cited as heroes, despite the fact that half the respondents were female."

Who is a hero? The late Christopher Reeve, who starred in the original Superman movies, gave a memorable definition. "A hero is an ordinary individual who finds strength to persevere and endure in spite of overwhelming obstacles."

What do heroes have in common? Listen to the comments made by today's heroes-movie stars, musicians or athletes. Most often they talk about themselves: who they are, what they have and why they are important. This self-focused attitude is the exact opposite of what it means to be a hero. True heroes display humility. They deflect praise from themselves.

Say something like:
Humility is a key character quality of all true heroes. What is humility? It is having a modest view of one's own worth. Philippians 2:3-4 states, "Do nothing out of selfish ambition or vain conceit, but in humility consider others better than yourselves. Each of you should look not only to your own interests, but also to the interests of others."

Ask:
What does humility have to do with being a hero?
What does Philippians 2:3-4 say we should and should not do?
How would you summarize Reeve's definition of a hero? (Break down this definition into its four key points.)

1. **Ordinary person**
2. **Finds strength**
3. **Perseveres and endures**
4. **Does so despite overwhelming odds**

Pride is defined as, "pleasure or satisfaction taken in an achievement, possession, or association." It is a natural human tendency that all of us possess. Every one of us struggles with humility. We are proud of our achievements and want others to recognize our worth. It is easy to look at what we have accomplished in order to feel good about ourselves. As Christians, this is a dangerous trap. Few things can hinder our relationship with God and our effectiveness as leaders faster than a prideful spirit.

Say something like:
Leadership is dangerous. It can corrupt. Many great leaders have fallen victim to the trap of sinful pride. It is easy for a leader who starts out with the best intentions to end up prideful. Many leaders allow their power to go to their heads and use it to abuse others. A leader who does not have humility will take all the credit, undermine their followers and in time drive the followers away. Leaders are people of humility. They are true heroes. As strong, effective leaders, they realize that their followers are their best asset and they actually deserve the credit for accomplishments.

Ask:
Why do leaders focus on others rather than themselves?
How is pride the opposite of humility?
How is pride a subtle trap?
When are you tempted to receive credit for the accomplishments of others?

Growing Deeper:

Jesus is the standard for humility. In an act of unbelievable humility, Jesus washed His disciples' feet. Think of it: God Himself willingly cleaned the dirt and stench from people's feet. Jesus calls His followers to follow His example. Intertwined with the experience is the message of love, forgiveness, servanthood and humility. As you read the following passages from John 13, consider the principles related to humility in leadership:

4...So (Jesus) got up from the meal, took off his outer clothing, and wrapped a towel around his waist. 5After that, he poured water into a basin and began to wash his disciples' feet, drying them with the towel that was wrapped around him ... 12When he had finished washing their feet, he put on his clothes and returned to his place. "Do you understand what I have done for you?" he asked them. 13"You call me 'Teacher' and 'Lord,' and rightly so, for that is what I am. 14Now that I, your Lord and Teacher, have washed your feet, you also should wash one another's feet. 15I have set you an example that you should do as I have done for you. 16I tell you the truth, no servant is greater than his master, nor is a messenger greater than the one who sent him. 17Now that you know these things, you will be blessed if you do them.

Ask:
How did Jesus demonstrate humility?
How would you have responded if Jesus wanted to wash your feet?
What principles do you learn from this passage that relate humility to leadership?

Listed below are possible answers:

1. Leaders have a vital **connection** with God.

2. Leaders **serve**; they are servants.

3. Leaders set the **example**.

4. Leaders are willing to do undesirable tasks.

5. Jesus set the example of **humility** in leadership.

6. Leaders will be **blessed** if they humbly serve others.

Note: You will use these principles in the following activity. You may wish to write them on a large sheet of paper for students to see.

"Take Two" Activity.

The goal of this activity is to compare and contrast prideful and humble responses to a variety of situations. Students will enjoy the exaggeration of this activity, but it will communicate a valuable point.

Instructions

Divide students into teams of 4-5 people. Give each team a different scenario and give them 10 minutes or less to create two skits-one that demonstrates humility; one that demonstrates a prideful response. Encourage creativity and exaggeration.

Remind students of the principles they learned from Jesus' example. Post the list of principles 1-6: 1. Leaders have a vital connection with God. 2. Leaders serve; they are servants. 3. Leaders set the example. 4. Leaders are willing to do undesirable tasks. 5. Jesus set the example of humility in leadership. 6. Leaders will be blessed if they humbly serve others.

Students must tell what "number" each skit reflects (or the opposite of it).

Scenarios:

You've just been invited to the best party ever. However, you soon discover your best friends are not on the guest list. How do you react when they ask you what you are doing this weekend?

Your teacher has just chosen you as the class leader for a fundraising project for a class trip. You are to assign every person in the class a role in the project and supervise them. But let's face it, some jobs are better than others. How do you decide who does what?

You and your friends both apply for the same summer job. You receive a phonecall that the company has hired you, but not your friends. How do you respond to this awkward situation?

You are in charge of a student worship service in two weeks. Some people will be front and center on stage and some will have to be working behind the scenes to plan the event. How do you decide who does what?

Your basketball team went from last place the year before to state champs this year. Local media is setting up a post-celebration interview with the whole team. How do you respond to their questions about your success?

You just became a Christian at a church event two months ago. Life's great, but now you are the only Christian in your family. How do you try to witness to your family about the change in your life?

Debrief with the following questions:

How well did the groups represent the principles of pride and humility?
Which attitude is usually second-nature-pride or humility? Why?

Lesson Summary:

- Humility is having a **modest** view of one's own worth.

- Humility is an **essential** quality for leaders.

- God is against the proud and **supports** the humble.

Optional Activity:

Instruct students to conduct a survey of 10 people who are not present today. Explain that you are taking a survey as part of a class assignment with no right or wrong answers. Ask them: Who is your hero and why? Record their answers and be prepared to share your findings in next week's meeting.

Lesson Four

Leaders are Humble

Introduction:
Humility is having a modest view of one's own worth; it is a key quality of leaders.

Going Public:
How comfortable would you be with someone calling you a hero?

Getting Focused:
"A hero is an ordinary individual who finds strength to persevere and endure in spite of overwhelming obstacles."

Definition of a Hero:

1. _____

2. _____

3. _____

4. _____

Growing Deeper:
Jesus is the standard for humility. In an act of unbelievable humility, Jesus washed his disciples' feet. Read John 13:1-7.

1. Leaders have a vital _____ with God.

2. Leaders _____; they are servants.

3. Leaders set the _____.

4. Leaders are willing to do _____ tasks.

5. Jesus set the example of _____ in leadership.

6. Leaders will be _____ if they humbly serve others.

Lesson Summary:

• Humility is having a _____ view of one's own worth.

• Humility is an _____ quality for leaders.

• God is against the proud and _____ the humble.

20

21

Lesson Five

Leaders Are Committed

Introduction:
Commitment is having a sincere and steadfast focus on a single purpose; it is a key quality of leaders. Once committed leaders begin something, they do not quit until they have accomplished their goal.

In this lesson, students will:
- Recognize the difference between being involvement and total commitment.
- Consider three important principles related to commitment.
- Study the challenge Moses presented to the Israelites regarding commitment.

Going Public:
When was a time you quit something when you should have stayed committed?

Note: You're looking for the most honest answer possible. Challenge students to "go public" with their fears and emotions as they relay their own personal experiences.

Expert Opinions:
"There are only two options regarding commitment. You're either IN or you're OUT. There's no such thing as life in between."
Pat Riley

"What people say, what people do, and what they say they do are entirely different things." *Margaret Meade*

"There's a difference between interest and commitment. When you're interested in doing something, you do it only when circumstances permit. When you're committed to something, you accept no excuses, only results." *Anonymous*

"People do not follow uncommitted leaders." *Stephen Gregg*

"Whatever you do, work at it with all your heart, as working for the Lord, not for men...." *Colossians 3:23*

Getting Focused:
To introduce this lesson, have students study the following quote and scripture about commitment:

"There are only two options regarding commitment. You're either IN or you're OUT. There's no such thing as life in between."
Pat Riley, Miami Heat Coach

"Whatever you do, work at it with all your heart, as working for the Lord, not for men...." *Colossians 3:23*

Ask:
How are these two quotes different?
How are they similar?
Why is it easier to work with your whole heart for God than for other people?

What is commitment? Here are two dictionary definitions: 1. the trait of sincere and steadfast focus on a single purpose; 2) the act of binding yourself (intellectually or emotionally) to a course of action.

Optional Activity

Select three readers for the following story-the narrator, the chicken and the pig. Have them read their parts in character. The narrator might sound wise and melodious. The chicken may use a high, screechy voice with appropriate chicken noises. Finally, the pig could use a low, bumbling voice with appropriate pig noises. Make the reading fun for everyone.

The story is told about the chicken and the pig who took a walk along a country road. It was a beautiful sunny day as they passed a group of children playing outside a house that was falling to pieces. The chicken said, "My ... it looks like those children haven't had a good meal in months." The pig replied, "It's just a shame that people live in such miserable circumstances, especially children." The chicken agreed and said, "I just wish there was something we could do about it." The two walked along in silence.

Suddenly the chicken had an idea. "Hey," offered the chicken, "I think there is something we can do to help them." The pig asked, "What do you have in mind?" "We can provide them with the best ham and egg breakfast they've ever eaten," the chicken said.

At first the pig agreed with the idea, but suddenly reality set in. "Now wait a minute," the pig gasped, "that menu is one-sided." The chicken asked, "What do you mean?" The pig stopped walking and said, "For you that means involvement, but for me it requires total commitment!"

Ask:
What is the point of this story?
What is the difference between involvement and total commitment?

Say something like:
People have their own definition of what it means to be committed to someone or something. Commitment boils down to three key principles.

    1. Commitment means **following through**.
    2. Commitment means: "**Say What You Mean and Mean What You Say**."
    3. Commitment means **being consistent, honest and trustworthy**.

1. Following Through

It's easy to dream, to set goals, to find amazing things to go after. People even start down the path towards their goal, but few actually achieve them. A goal without follow through is just a dream.

Pair and Share:

Select a partner and spend 1 minute each discussing the following question:

- What things cause people to quit their goals mid-stream?

2. "Say What You Mean and Mean What You Say."

Disappointment happens all the time. People make promises they don't intend to keep. They commit to doing things and change their mind at the last minute. It happens all the time, but this must not define your character.

Ask (the entire group):
Why is it important to keep promises?
Do others know you as a man/woman of your word? Why or why not?

3. Be Consistent, Honest, Trustworthy

Leaders are called to a different standard. They must keep their word at all times. The primary reason is trust. No one will follow you if they don't trust you. People must trust you completely in order to follow you.

Ask (the entire group):
Why do you trust the leaders you are following in your life right now?

Share the following quotation from President Teddy Roosevelt who offered this advice to leaders regarding commitment:

"It is not the critic who counts; not the man who points out how the strong man stumbles or where the doer of deeds could have done better. The credit belongs to the man who is actually in the arena, whose face is marred by dust and sweat and blood, who strives valiantly, who errs and comes up short again and again, because there is no effort without error or short-coming, but who knows the great enthusiasms, the great devotions, who spends himself for a worthy cause; who, at best, knows, in the end, the triumph of high achievement, and who, at the worst, if he fails, at least he fails while daring greatly, so that his place shall never be with those cold and timid souls who knew neither victory nor defeat."

Ask:
Why don't critics count?
Who is the person "in the arena?"
Why are things so hard for that person?
What rewards will he experience?

Leaders provide a spark when the team slows down. They push when others don't want to go on. If students set an example in this area, they will stand apart from the crowd and others will follow. They will set the standard that others aspire to achieve.

Growing Deeper:

Commitment is making a choice and sticking with it no matter what. Right before Moses died, he presented a clear choice to the people of Israel. As you read the passage in Deuteronomy 30:15-18, list the principles related to commitment in leadership:

15See, I set before you today life and prosperity, death and destruction. 16For I command you today to love the LORD your God, to walk in his ways, and to keep his commands, decrees and laws; then you will live and increase, and the LORD your God will bless you in the land you are entering to possess. 17But if your heart turns away and you are not obedient, and if you are drawn away to bow down to other gods and worship them, 18I declare to you this day that you will certainly be destroyed. You will not live long in the land you are crossing the Jordan to enter and possess.

Ask:
What were their two choices?
How did God define total commitment for His people?
What principles do you learn from this passage about commitment and leadership?

Listed below are possible answers:

Commitment is a choice.

Choosing God's way results in life and prosperity.

Choosing any other way results in death and destruction.

Say something like:
Our commitment to Christ must be more than involvement in Christian activities; it must begin to involve sacrificing our time, talent and treasure. Jesus asks for total commitment-all we have and all we are.

"Winning the Tug of War" Activity
The purpose of this activity is for students to experience half-hearted vs. total commitment. Please be safety conscious!

Instructions
Divide students into four equal teams. Each team will participate in a tug-of-war contest.

Round 1   Match #1: Team A will compete against Team B.

Match #2: Team C will battle Team D.

Each team selects a captain who will position the players as desired. The captains will go over the rules privately with their respective teams. The winner of each contest is the team whose members demonstrate the greatest degree of commitment to the cause.

Round 2   Match #1: The winners of Round 1 contend against each other.

Match #2: The runners-up of Round 1 contend against each other.

Round 3

Privately give the following instructions to the team captains. Remind the captain to go over the rules privately with their respective team.

Instructions for...Teams A & C:

Do your best

Don't give up

Work together

Encourage others

Be a good sport

Team B:

> Pull hard to start
>
> The Captain will count "1...2...3"
>
> On 3, stop pulling

Team D:

> Boys: don't pull at all throughout
>
> Girls: pull hard throughout

Vary the matches so that the various "instructions" create tension between the teams.

Debrief by asking:

Did you figure out which teams had what instructions?
What did this activity teach you about full and half-hearted commitment?
What was difficult about this activity?
What would have made victory more certain?

Close this lesson with a meaningful time for students to envision their commitment to the team and to the leadership development process. Ask students to close their eyes and envision themselves at this same time next year. Using their imagination, ask them to picture the following: How have they grown as a leader over the past 12 months? What new ministries might they be in charge of? What demonstrations of God's power have they seen during the past year? How many people have come to know Christ in the past year as a result? Pray aloud for each student's vision regarding the impact of their own personal leadership over the next year.

Lesson Summary:

- Commitment means following through.

- Commitment means: "Say What You Mean and Mean What You Say."

- Commitment means being consistent, honest, and trustworthy.

LeaderTreks

Lesson Five

Leaders Are Committed

Introduction:
Once committed leaders begin something, they do not quit until they have accomplished their goal.

Going Public:
When was a time you quit something when you should have stayed committed?

Getting Focused:

1. Commitment means _____ _____.

2. Commitment means: _____ _____.

3. Commitment menas _____ _____.

"It is not the critic who counts; not the man who points out how the strong man stumbles or where the doer of deeds could have done better. The credit belongs to the man who is actually in the arena, whose face is marred by dust and sweat and blood, who strives valiantly, who errs and comes up short again and again, because there is no effort without error or shortcoming, but who knows the great enthusiasms, the great devotions, who spends himself for a worthy cause; who, at best, knows, in the end, the triumph of high achievement, and who, at the worst, if he fails, at least he fails while daring greatly, so that his place shall never be with those cold and timid souls who knew neither victory nor defeat." *-President Teddy Roosevelt*

Growing Deeper:
Read Deuteronomy 30:15-18. Moses presented the people of Israel with an opportunity to fully devote themselves to God.

Lesson Summary:
- Commitment means following through.

- Commitment means: "Say What You Mean and Mean What You Say."

- Commitment means being consistent, honest, and trustworthy.

Lesson Six

Leaders are Obedient

Introduction:
Obedience is the act of carrying out a command or order; it is a key quality of leaders. Leaders have no problem answering to God and/or other people in authority.

In this lesson, students will:
- Understand obedience as an essential quality of leaders.
- Consider how obedience relates to our trusting relationship with God.
- Learn about how obedience relates to faith, love, submission and blessing by studying the life of Jesus.

Going Public:
When was a time you chose disobedience over obedience (to God, to parents, etc.), and what was the result?

Note: You're looking for the most honest answer possible. Challenge students to "go public" with their fears and emotions as they relay their own personal experiences.

Expert Opinions:
"One act of obedience is better than one hundred sermons" *Dietrich Bonhoeffer*

"The ship that will not obey the helm will have to obey the rocks." *English Proverb*

"Obedience does not require understanding, but it does require trust." *Unknown*

"Understanding can wait. Obedience cannot." *Geoffrey Grogan*

"Whoever has my commands and obeys them, he is the one who loves me. He who loves me will be loved by my Father, and I too will love him and show myself to him." *John 14:21*

Getting Focused:
To introduce this lesson to students, write on a big piece of paper before the meeting starts: "DO NOT SIT DOWN!" Don't explain why and don't try to enforce the rule.

When it is time to begin your meeting, introduce the topic of the lesson by saying something like:

Some of you may have figured out the topic of today's lesson-obedience. Some of you saw the sign and did exactly as told, without knowing why. Some of you questioned it. Some of you may have even gone against it and sat down anyway. Obedience is the act of carrying out a command or order, without necessarily knowing why. The choice on whether or not to comply lies solely with the recipient of the command or order.

Have a student volunteer read the following two quotes:

"One act of obedience is better than one hundred sermons." *Dietrich Bonhoeffer, author martyred for his faith*

"Understanding can wait. Obedience cannot." *Geoffrey Grogan, Principal Emeritus of Glasgow Bible College*

Ask:
How would you rephrase these quotes in your own words?

Share the following true illustration:

A child of missionary parents in Zaire, Africa loved to play in the family's front yard. One day while playing near a tree the youngster's father frantically screamed from the porch, "Stop!" The child immediately stopped and felt a wave of fear. "Obey me instantly," the father yelled. "Drop to your stomach!"

(pause the story) Ask:
Imagine you are this child. What would you do in this situation and why?
What thoughts would be going through your mind?
Why do you think the father yelled at his child?

(Note: Most students will say that they would obey their father because something is wrong. Some may think the father is mad because they did something wrong. Continue the story below.)

Instantly the youngster did as the father commanded. "Now crawl toward me as fast as you can!" The child obeyed and quickly scrambled on hands and knees toward him. In a moment, the father then urgently said, "Now, stand up and run straight to me!" The child responded at once and jumped into the father's arms. Turning around to find out about the danger, the child saw a large poisonous snake dangling from a branch-inches from where he had been playing!

Ask:
What could have been the child's response?
What could have happened if the child did not respond as the father asked?
Do you need to know why before you obey? Explain.
What does this story have to do with leadership?

Say something like:
Most likely you are used to being told what to do. Your parents tell you, "Clean up your room." Your teacher says, "Don't forget to do your homework." The coach announces, "Run another lap around the field." The boss warns, "Don't be late for work." Leaders are not always in charge-they have to be good followers who respect and respond to authority.

The way leaders respond to the commands of people in authority over them says a great deal about their character. Godly obedience occurs immediately, willingly and joyfully. Philippians 2:5 says, "Your attitude should be the same as that of Christ Jesus." Verse 8 in that same passage reminds us that Jesus "...humbled himself and became obedient to death- even death on a cross!" So what else can we learn about obedience from Jesus?

Growing Deeper:

1. First, Jesus showed us that obedience is based on faith. In faith, He went to the cross because He trusted His Father. The child in the story obeyed the father in faith and without hesitation. The relationship leaders have with God is the same. They obey Him because they trust Him. Similarly, followers only obey leaders they trust.

Read Luke 9:51. Ask:

What event awaited Jesus in Jerusalem?
Why was He so focused on going there even though he knew what was ahead of Him (suffering and death)?

2. A second truth is that obedience demonstrates love. The child in the story was certain of the father's love and obeyed without question. Leaders obey God because they know He loves them, and their obedience shows God that they love Him, too. Likewise, followers thrive when they know their leader loves them.

Read John 14:21a. Ask:
Who obeys Jesus?

3. Third, Jesus demonstrated that obedience requires submission. In the illustration, the child submitted to the father's will without complaint. Leaders must submit to God's authority if they expect followers to submit to their leadership. The father in Zaire commanded the child do four things: drop, crawl, stand and run. None of these orders made sense, but the child took these actions without understanding. Leaders must submit to and obey God though they don't understand everything. Correspondingly, followers must do their part even when don't see the big picture.

Read Matthew 26:42. Ask:
How much courage does it take to pray Jesus' prayer?

4. Fourth, Jesus illustrated that obedience brings blessing. Obedience is a choice with logical consequences either way. In the example, the child's entire future came down to a choice: obey and live, or disobey and die. Leaders who obey experience the abundant life, as do their followers. Leaders who disobey cut themselves off from God with negative effects for their followers.

Read John 13:17. Ask:
Is it enough to know Jesus' commands? Why or why not?

"Shipmates" Activity

This team activity will illustrate the principle of trust involved in obedience.

Equipment:

> One paper bag per team
>
> Lots of large and small items
>
> Blindfolds

Instructions

Form pairs. One partner in each pair is blindfolded and holds a paper bag. All blindfolded partners line up single file with their partners standing next to them. Each pair will compete against other pairs in one-minute rounds. The goal is to gather as many objects scattered on the floor as possible in one minute.

The "sighted" players will guide their partners to the objects using only verbal commands. Physical contact is not allowed between any players. After one minute, each pair will receive one point for each item in their bag. The winner is the team with the most points after all team pairs have competed.

Switch roles. The competition remains the same except this time the "sighted" players can't use words to guide their blindfolded players to the objects.

Debrief by asking:

What did your partner do right? How could he/she improve?
What did this illustration teach you about obedience?
Is obedience blind? Why or why not?

Close this lesson by challenging students to examine every area of obedience to authority in their lives. This includes parents, teachers, employers, church leadership and law enforcement officers (speeding, etc.). Encourage them to review their current level of quick and unquestioning obedience in each area. Pray with them and for them about these areas and hold them accountable over the coming weeks.

Lesson Summary:
- Obedience is **based** on faith
- Obedience **demonstrates** love.
- Obedience **requires** submission.
- Obedience **brings** blessing.

LeaderTreks

Leadership365

Lesson Six

Leaders Are Obedient

Lesson Summary:
- Obedience is _____ on faith
- Obedience _____ love.
- Obedience _____ submission.
- Obedience _____ blessing.

Introduction:
Obedience is the act of carrying out a command or order; it is a key quality of leaders.

Going Public:
When was a time you chose disobedience over obedience (to God, to parents, etc.), and what was the result?

Getting Focused:
The way leaders respond to the commands of people in authority over them says a great deal about their character. Godly obedience occurs immediately, willingly, and joyfully.

Growing Deeper:
Read Luke 9:51.

1. _____

Read John 14:21a.

2. _____

Read Matthew 26:42.

3. _____

Read John 13:17.

4. _____

24

25

Lesson Seven

Leaders Are Courageous

Introduction:
Courage is what enables one to face danger, fear, or trials with confidence, resolution, and bravery. It is not just the absence of fear in our lives; courage is having the strength, power and might to be different. Courage is standing up for what is right, no matter what the consequences.

In this lesson, students will:
Understand courage is facing and dealing with anything dangerous, difficult or painful, rather than withdrawing from it.

Learn the value of standing up for what is right regardless of the consequences.

Consider how courage develops through your relationship with God, walking into your fears and persevering through difficulties.

Consider an example of courageous leadership from the Book of Daniel.

Going Public:
What is the most courageous thing you've ever done?

Note: You're looking for the most honest answer possible. Challenge students to "go public" with their fears and emotions as they relay their own personal experiences.

Expert Opinions:
"Courage is contagious. When a brave man takes a stand, the spines of others are stiffened." *Billy Graham*

"One man with courage makes a majority." *Andrew Jackson*

"It often requires more courage to dare to do right than to fear to do wrong." *Abraham Lincoln*

"Courage does not always roar. Sometimes it is the quiet voice at the end of the day saying, 'I will try again tomorrow.' " *Unknown*

"Have I not commanded you? Be strong and courageous. Do not be terrified; do not be discouraged, for the LORD your God will be with you wherever you go." *Joshua 1:9*

Getting Focused:
To introduce this lesson to students, say something like:

Have you ever been really scared? I'm not talking about a haunted house or scary movies. I'm talking about "afraid for your life" and "think you're going to die at any moment" scared. Fear provides a unique form of clarity for us. When you are really afraid you instinctively understand what is truly important.

Share the following illustration:

A four year old boy fell off a small roller coaster in a neighbor's backyard. Consequently, he developed an intense fear of roller coasters. Thirty years later, his ten year old son wanted to spend a "day with Dad" at an amusement park. The moment they entered the gates, his son ran as fast as he could to the park's legendary rickety wooden roller coaster. How could the dad disappoint his son?

They got in a car-the front car-and strapped themselves in. The ride began and the car climbed the first steep incline. On the left-hand side was a small building housing the power and controls for the roller coaster. The father calculated the odds of surviving a jump onto the roof of the building.

At that instant, his son said, "Dad, isn't this great?" The man thought, "Yeah, just great!" During this momentary distraction, the father missed his chance to bail out and was irreversibly committed to the ride. They reached the apex and for an instant, the car seemed to hang in thin air before it lurched downward. They hurtled toward earth at dizzying speeds with the father screaming all the way to the bottom.

Incredibly, something happened as they finished their first descent and climbed toward the second assault. The man started to enjoy himself, at least enough to stop screaming at the top of his lungs.

When the ride ended, the son jumped out of the car and said, "Dad, let's go again." The two of them went on the ride six times in a row. By the end of the day, the pair had gone on every coaster in the park, and father and son had built a memory that would last for the rest of their lives. Something else happened, too. By walking into his fear, the man overcame it.

Ask:
Have you ever had a similar experience of overcoming a fear? Explain.
What does courage have to do with leadership?

Perhaps the most important ingredient in developing courage is facing one's fears. Everyone fears something or someone. The question is not, "What or whom do you fear?" The real question is, "What do you do with your fears?" Leaders who willingly walk into their fears find that once faced, the fear no longer look so fearsome.

The furnace of affliction is the surest way to forge a courageous heart. When life is tough, courageous leaders faithfully persevere through the storm finding strength and shelter in the arms of God. Drawing on His resources, courageous leaders eventually prevail. How do leaders develop greater courage? It begins with the quality of one's personal relationship with God. Courageous leaders learn to live a consistent life of constant devotion to God in all circumstances. The more time they spend connected with Christ the more transformation that occurs in their character and conduct. Over time, they learn to submit their selfish will to the selfless will of their loving Father. God is calling for courageous leaders to go out and change the world. Are you ready?

Six-Day Journal Exercise
We naturally avoid fear-experiencing it or even talking about it. Sometimes we are most afraid of what God will "do" to us if we fully commit to Him. God can change our timid hearts, but only if we focus on the root issues of what scares us about following him more closely. Encourage students to take the next six days to journal their thoughts about courage and fear. Provoke their thinking by using the following questions:

What are my core fears in life right now?
How do I know when a relationship or situation has tapped into one of those core fears? How do I typically respond?
What is my greatest fear about following God more closely?
What do I fear most about being a leader for Christ?
What hope and help can I find in God's Word to strengthen my courage? (list several scriptures and meditate on them)

Optional Activity:

Journal with a partner. Be vulnerable to one another and pray for each other as you discuss your fears. Take the next six days as a short journey through your core fears and see what God teaches you on the other side of this experience.

Growing Deeper:

True courage is not only about standing up in the face of danger, but also standing firm on your convictions. Courageous leaders choose to stand for God's truth despite unusual trials, unfair attacks and unexpected persecution. Through it all, courageous leaders remain consistent in their determination to stand for what is right. They live life outside the bounds of what is considered "normal." The fire of their personality kindles a spark in the souls of the lives they touch.

Read Daniel 3: 16-19, 23-27 and then list at least one principle concerning courageous leadership.

16Shadrach, Meshach and Abednego replied to the king, "O Nebuchadnezzar, we do not need to defend ourselves before you in this matter. 17If we are thrown into the blazing furnace, the God we serve is able to save us from it, and he will rescue us from your hand, O king. 18But even if he does not, we want you to know, O king, that we will not serve your gods or worship the image of gold you have set up." 19Then Nebuchadnezzar was furious with Shadrach, Meshach and Abednego, and his attitude toward them changed. He ordered the furnace heated seven times hotter than usual ... 23and these three men, firmly tied, fell into the blazing furnace. 24Then King Nebuchadnezzar leaped to his feet in amazement and asked his advisers, "Weren't there three men that we tied up and threw into the fire?" They replied, "Certainly, O king." 25He said, "Look! I see four men walking around in the fire, unbound and unharmed, and the fourth looks like a son of the gods."... 27They saw that the fire had not harmed their bodies, nor was a hair of their heads singed; their robes were not scorched, and there was no smell of fire on them.

Ask:
How do you think Daniel defined true courage?
In whom was Daniel's confidence?
Does courage always equal experiencing success? Why or why not?
What other principles of leadership and courage do you learn from this passage?

Listed below are principles related to courage in leadership.

    1. Leaders stand firm on what they know to be true despite consequences.

    2. Leaders are willing to pay the price for taking a stand for what is right.

    3. Leaders are being watched carefully, especially in crisis situations.

    4. Leaders know that God is with them in the midst of crisis.

Video Clip: Gettysburg (1993)

Show the following two clips from Gettysburg:

Scene 29: Bracing for siege {3:50}

Scene 35: Bayonets [3:13]

Total Time: 7:03

Say something like:
The bloodiest war in our nation's history was the Civil War (1861-1865). The turning point of the war was the Battle of Gettysburg fought on July 1-3, 1863. Colonel Joshua Lawrence Chamberlain commanded the 20th Maine Volunteer Infantry Regiment. His leadership in defending the strategic site called Little Big Top was one of the keys to the Union victory.

As you watch the video clips from the movie Gettysburg (1993) focus on the leadership of Colonel Chamberlain, played by actor Jeff Bridges.

Ask:
In what ways was Colonel Chamberlain an effective leader?
How did Colonel Chamberlain embody courageous leadership?

Close this lesson with a special time of prayer. Circle up. (Provide each student with a small rock prior to your prayer time. River rocks are available at most craft stores.) Tell students that this rock represents a core fear in their lives. Give them a few moments to define what that fear is (silently or, if the group has time, share it with the group). Tell students to clench the rock in their fists very tightly. Notice how the harder they clench their "fear" that it begins to have negative consequences. It may hurt. Their fists may turn white. Now, have them release their grip. Releasing our fears to God is such a relief. Have students drop their "fears" in a pile in the center of the circle, symbolizing they will leave their deepest fear in God's care. Close in prayer.

Lesson Summary:
- Courage enables one to face danger, fear or trials with **confidence**, **resolution** and **bravery**.
- Courage develops through your **relationship** with God, walking into your fears and persevering through **difficulties**.

From The Student Guide

LeaderTreks Leadership365

Lesson Seven

Leaders Are Courageous

Introduction:
Courage is what enables one to face danger, fear, or trials with confidence, resolution, and bravery.

Going Public:
What is the most courageous thing you've ever done?

Getting Focused:
Six-Day Journal Exercise

- What are my core fears in life right now?
- How do I know when a relationship or situation has tapped into one of those core fears? How do I typically respond?
- What is my greatest fear about following God more closely?
- What do I fear most about being a leader for Christ?
- What hope and help can I find in God's Word to strengthen my courage? (list several scriptures and meditate on them)

26   27

LeaderTreks   Leadership365

Growing Deeper:
Read Daniel 3:16-19, 23-27.

1. Leaders stand firm on what they know to be true regardless of consequences.
2. Leaders are willing to pay the price for taking a stand for what is right.
3. Leaders are being watched carefully, especially in crisis situations.
4. Leaders know that God is with them in the midst of crisis.

Lesson Summary:
- Courage enables one to face dangers, fears or trials with _____, _____ and _____.
- Courage develops through your _____ with God, walking into your fears, and _____ through difficulties.

32   33

Lesson Eight

Leaders Are Compassionate

Introduction:

Compassion is a desire to free others from suffering. Sometimes compassion takes the form of forgiving others and demonstrating mercy. At other times, compassion means doing what you can to help someone less fortunate.

In this lesson, students will:

- Understand God's definition of compassion and Jesus' example of compassion.

- Examine biblical principles related to compassion through the story of the Good Samaritan.

- Develop an action plan to assist a neighboring town in crisis.

Going Public:

Other than Jesus, who is the most compassionate person you know, and why?

Note: You're looking for the most honest answer possible. Challenge students to "go public" with their fears and emotions as they relay their own personal experiences.

Expert Opinions:

"The purpose of human life is to serve and show compassion and the will to help others." *Albert Schweitzer*

"Life's most urgent question is, what are you doing for others?" *Martin Luther King, Jr*

"It is lack of love for ourselves that inhibits our compassion toward others. If we make friends with ourselves, then there is no obstacle to opening our hearts and minds to others." *Unknown*

"It's not how much we give, but how much love we put in the doing - that's compassion in action." *Mother Teresa*

"Praise be to the God and Father of our Lord Jesus Christ, the Father of compassion and the God of all comfort, who comforts us in all our troubles, so that we can comfort those in any trouble with the comfort we ourselves have received from God." *2 Corinthians 1:3-4*

Getting Focused:

To introduce this lesson to students, focus on the following quotation by Martin Luther King Jr.:

"Life's most urgent question is, 'What are you doing for others?'" *Martin Luther King, Jr*

Ask:
What are you doing for others?

Have students form pairs and spend one minute each discussing this question.

Say something like:
Compassion toward others is not a natural emotion. We often have to fight to take the focus off of ourselves and consider another person's situation. We may feel sorry for someone who is hurting, but a leader's compassion is much more than emotion. Compassion is mercy in action. It is what motivates us to do something about a person's plight.

Introduce the following story by asking students these questions:

How many of you are planning to attend college?
How many of your families have been setting aside money for your college education?

The Christian parents of three small children started a college fund soon after their first child was born. They regularly put money into their savings account so their children could attend high quality institutions of higher learning.

A family friend with a reputation for integrity offered to invest the family's college fund for them. The parents agreed and soon their college fund was doing better than ever. By the time the first child graduated from high school, the college fund already had enough money to pay for all three children's education-on paper.

When the parents tried to withdraw funds for the tuition, the adviser told them that there would be a slight delay. The paperwork authorizing the wire transfer took several days to process. Two days went by. Three days. Four. No money.

The news story broke at the end of the week. A grand jury had indicted their friend on numerous counts of fraud. The money in the college fund was gone. At trial the jury found the financial advisor guilty and the judge sentenced the man to 10 years in prison. The convicted felon lost his family and friends, his house and possessions, his dignity and reputation.

(pause the story) Ask:
If this happened to you, and you lost your money because a friend committed fraud, how would you react?

Initially the family was shocked, angry and devastated. They wanted their money back, but it was long gone. They wanted answers concerning the crime, and there were none. In their view, the man got what he deserved and was fortunate that he hadn't received a stiffer sentence.

Over time, however, their hurt and anger diminished, and God began to change their hearts. The parents decided to forgive the man and to support him during his confinement. Thereafter, the family called the prisoner, wrote letters to him and the father visited him in prison weekly. After his release from prison, the family helped the man find housing and employment. Of all the people the ex-con knew, this family was the only one that didn't turn their backs on him. This is a true story of compassion in action.

Ask:
How does this story illustrate compassion?
What does this story have to do with leadership?
Why does it take a strong leader to practice forgiveness?

Say something like:
The dictionary defines compassion as a "deep awareness of the suffering of another coupled with the wish to relieve it." Others define compassion as "a desire to free others from their suffering." As Christians, we experience God's compassion moment by moment because of forgiveness through Christ. As a result of what He did for us, He expects us not to withhold compassion from others. He commands us to forgive others as we ourselves have been forgiven. Sometimes this is easier said than done!

We understand compassion better when we model our lives after the example of the Son of God. Throughout the Gospels we catch glimpses of Jesus' heart of compassion. Have students take turns reading the following scriptures and comment on what each verse teaches us about Jesus' compassion.

"When he saw the crowds, he had compassion on them, because they were harassed and helpless, like sheep without a shepherd" (Matthew 9:36).

"When Jesus landed and saw a large crowd, he had compassion on them and healed their sick" (Matthew 14:14).

"Filled with compassion, Jesus reached out his hand and touched the man. 'I am willing,' he said. 'Be clean!'" (Mark 1:41).

"I have compassion for these people; they have already been with me three days and have nothing to eat" (Mark 8:2).

What does a compassionate leader look like? Through Jesus' example, we see:

1. Compassion is the motive of a leader's heart. He served out of the deep compassion He felt for others. He saw their desperate needs and determined to help meet those needs.

2. Compassion is the perspective of a leader's eyes. When He looked at a broken world He saw broken hearts and lives, and His heart was broken for hurting people.

3. Compassion is the magnet of a leader's heart. Every moment, Jesus' heartbeat was to see wrongs righted, hurts healed, suffering alleviated and sinners saved.

4. Compassion is the action of a leader's hands and feet. Jesus didn't just feel sad about heartache; He did something about it! He took action and became personally involved in the lives of others.

Compassion was the basis of Jesus' mission statement-His reason for being on earth. "For the Son of Man came to seek and to save what was lost" (Luke 19:10). Remarkably, these words flowed from the lips of a holy God who demands justice, yet took our punishment upon Himself out of His deep compassion.

Say something like:
We can summarize these principles this way:

- Compassion = our **motive**

- Compassion = our **perspective**

- Compassion = our **magnet**

- Compassion = our **action**

- Compassion = our **mission**

Growing Deeper:

Read Luke 10:30-37. What leadership principles can you glean from this passage about leadership and compassion?

30In reply Jesus said: "A man was going down from Jerusalem to Jericho, when he fell into the hands of robbers. They stripped him of his clothes, beat him and went away, leaving him half dead. 31A priest happened to be going down the same road, and when he saw the man, he passed by on the other side. 32So too, a Levite, when he came to the place and saw him, passed by on the other side. 33But a Samaritan, as he traveled, came where the man was; and when he saw him, he took pity on him. 34He went to him and bandaged his wounds, pouring on oil and wine. Then he put the man on his own donkey, took him to an inn and took care of him. 35The next day he took out two silver coins and gave them to the innkeeper. 'Look after him,' he said, 'and when I return, I will reimburse you for any extra expense you may have.' 36"Which of these three do you think was a neighbor to the man who fell into the hands of robbers?" 37The expert in the law replied, "The one who had mercy on him." Jesus told him, "Go and do likewise." Luke 10:30-37

Consider the additional list below of principles related to compassion in leadership:

1. Leaders know that **everyone** faces hard times.

2. Leaders don't **ignore** suffering.

3. Leaders show compassion to those in **need**.

4. Leaders take **action** to relieve suffering.

5. Leaders go **the extra mile** to help others.

Ask:

When was a time you had mercy on someone who didn't deserve it?
How would you describe your general level of compassion toward others? Ask students to reflect on their answer(s) silently.
a. I look for opportunities to show mercy to others
b. I will show compassion when someone guilts me into doing it.
c. It's hard for me to show mercy to others-especially if it's undeserved
d. I don't think much about being compassionate toward others until an obvious need comes along like a fundraiser for
   world hunger or a mission project
e. I try to show compassion to others because of God's mercy towards me

"Seaside Mission" Activity

This activity will show students that compassion is not just emotion-it is mercy translated into action. The goal of this initiative is for students to develop a realistic plan of assistance to those in need.

Instructions

Divide students into teams of four people each. Imagine that you live in a town along the eastern seaboard. A hurricane caused minor damage in your town, but it destroyed a coastal town 30 miles away. People have no shelter, no running water, no electricity and little means of transportation in or out of the city. The governor has declared martial law in the neighboring town. No outsiders are permitted in the town so you cannot physically assist in the cleanup and rebuilding.

You are an officer on the Executive Board of your student council. As a group, decide who will play which positions: president, vice-president, recording secretary and/ or treasure. Your mission is to develop an action plan to provide "hands-on" assistance in this crisis to the residents of the neighboring town. What specifically would each person do in each role to help these people?

Give students 12-15 minutes to come up with a plan. Students must be able to summarize their general idea in a two-minute speech to present for the group. The group must "vote" on which plan best demonstrates the elements of compassion and has the best chance of success.

Optional Activity:

Sometimes the Holy Spirit will convict students in the area of compassion and you will need to help them respond to His leading. For some, the need is close to home-they may have a specific family member or friend in mind that needs their compassion. Others may want to become more involved in world missions or local service projects. Be sensitive to God's leading in this area. Close by asking students to pray about what God wants them to do next as a result of this lesson.

Lesson Summary:

- Compassion is the motive of a leader's heart.

- Compassion is the perspective of a leader's eyes.

- Compassion is the beat of a leader's heart.

- Compassion is the action of a leader's hands and feet.

From The Student Guide

Lesson Eight

Leaders Are Compassionate

Lesson Summary:
- Compassion is the motive of a leader's heart.
- Compassion is the perspective of a leader's eyes.
- Compassion is the beat of a leader's heart.
- Compassion is the action of a leader's hands and feet.

Introduction:
Compassion is a desire to free others from suffering.

Going Public:
Other than Jesus, who is the most compassionate person you know, and why?

Getting Focused:
- Compassion = our _____
- Compassion = our _____
- Compassion = our _____
- Compassion = our _____
- Compassion = our _____

Growing Deeper:
Read Luke 10:30-37.

1. Leaders know that _____ faces hard times.

2. Leaders don't _____ suffering.

3. Leaders show compassion to those in _____.

4. Leaders take _____ to relieve suffering.

5. Leaders go _____ to help others.

34

35

Section Four:
The Tasks and Responsibilities of Leaders

Semester Two

When it's time for action, the world expects leaders to know what to do. Effective leaders will act quickly and decisively because they have developed the skills necessary to lead their team toward success.

Lesson One

Doing Flows out of Being

Introduction:
Doing flows out of being, not the other way around. Leaders lead from the heart-a heart that God is constantly transforming to be like His. If you know who a leader is supposed to be (in terms of godly character), it's easier to determine what a leader is supposed to do. Doing flows out of being.

In this lesson, students will:
- Understand the two sides of leadership-doing and being.
- Examine how Scripture illustrates the two sides of leadership
- Decide to develop their character in order to make an impact on God's kingdom.

Going Public:
When was a time you tried acting a certain way that wasn't consistent with who you really are?

Note: You're looking for the most honest answer possible. Challenge students to "go public" with their fears and emotions as they relay their own personal experiences.

Getting Focused:
(To introduce this lesson to students, you will want to have several dimes to distribute to students.)

Say something like:
According to the Cambridge Dictionary of American Idioms the phrase, "two sides of the same coin" refers to "different but closely related features of one idea." For example, comedy and tragedy are two sides of the same coin. Both are closely related to theatrical arts, but they represent two ways of looking at the world and two ways of living in it. Last semester, we studied one side of leadership-being a godly person who is prepared to lead. This semester, we are going to study how to act like a leader because "doing" leadership flows out of first "being" a leader people want to follow. Let's start by looking at the two sides of an actual coin-a United States dime.

Have students select a partner for this 10-minute exercise. Ask them to:

> 1. Study the "heads" side of the coin above and make a list of observations.
>
> 2. Study the "tails" side of the coin above and make a list of observations.
>
> 3. Compare the two lists. What is similar about the two sides? What is different?

After students have a chance to share their observations, ask the group:

> Why are there two sides to the coin?
>
> Which side is the coin? Explain your answer.
>
> Which part of leadership is most important-doing or being? Explain.

(Note: Encourage students to realize that both sides are equally important.)

Optional Activity

Host an informal debate on doing vs. being as it relates to leadership. Divide students into two teams. Give them 10 minutes to prepare their points and then ask students to debate each other on the question: What part of leadership is most important-doing or being? Allow several pairs of students debate each other in 2-minute rounds.

There are two sides to leadership: doing and being. The doing side is what leaders do; the being side is who leaders are. The doing side relates to the leader's conduct and actions; the being side refers to the leader's character and attitudes.

Read Psalm 78:72. This verse spells out these two sides of leadership.

> "And David shepherded them with integrity of heart; with skillful hands he led them."

Ask:

How does this verse characterize David as a leader?

David was the shepherd of Israel; this describes his role as a leader.)

How does this verse capture both sides of leadership?

(He had integrity; this relates to his character as a leader. He had skills; this involves his conduct as a leader.)

We can learn three important points about leadership from this verse:

1. Leaders are <u>shepherds</u>.
Ask:
What does a literal shepherd do?
What does a shepherd-leader do?

They guide, direct, serve, protect, nurture and care for their followers. They stand before people pointing the way to the future and serving as an example for others to follow. Leaders model themselves after Jesus, the Good Shepherd who laid down His life for the sheep.

2. Leaders have <u>integrity</u>.

Ask:
What is your definition of integrity?
How can you develop greater integrity?

They know that leadership involves being. The person they are in private is the same person they are in public. They say what they mean and mean what they say. They are not perfect, but they are becoming more like Jesus every day by carefully cultivating their relationship with Him.

3. Leaders have <u>skills</u>.

Ask:
How would you complete this sentence about leadership skills: You cannot be a leader if you don't know how to _____
_____.

What top two skills do you possess that relate to leadership? (limit responses to two or three students)

Leaders know that leadership involves doing. They take action by employing their leadership skills. Actions truly do speak louder than words. When the chance comes to stand for the truth no matter the cost, leaders are first to rise to the challenge.

Say something like:
Read Psalm 78:72 again. We know it teaches two sides of leadership. But what came first in David's life: being or doing? Let's take a closer look.

Growing Deeper:

First and foremost, David had "integrity of heart." Then he used his "skillful hands" to lead them. Character comes before conduct; being comes before doing. A key leadership principle is simply, "Being flows out of doing, not the other way around." Who you are as a person affects everything you do as a leader. Aim to be a person of character first; then your actions will naturally align with God's purposes.

Split students into pairs. Have students look up the following scriptures that focus on character, but encourage them to focus on what someone like this does as a result.

Ask:
Based on these verses, what could someone of character "do" to impact God's kingdom?

      Philippians 2:14

      Colossians 1:10

      2 Timothy 2:15

      James 1:19-20

      1 Peter 1:15

Say something like:
What has God called you to do for Him to make a difference? He is preparing your heart to "be" somebody who "does" something significant for His kingdom. The world believes the bottom line for leaders is their performance. The measure of leadership from the world's perspective is whether or not leaders meet or exceed their goals. Make no mistake. It's important for leaders to do a good job-especially for leaders who are Christ followers. Poor performance will undermine the authority of every leader. However, it takes a leader with godly character in order to know and to do the right thing.

Read the following humorous quote and ask for students to respond to it.

"Always do right. This will gratify some people - and astonish the rest." *Mark Twain*

"Quick Line Up" Activity
The goal is for leadership to emerge naturally among the students in order to accomplish the task at a fast pace.

Instructions

Divide students into two teams. The two large teams should form two lines facing each other. Listen for a command. When given, line up as quickly as possible. The first team to complete the command is the winner. The overall winner is the team that wins 4 of 7 competitions.

Commands (you may add more):

Say: Line up by...

1. Alphabetical by first or last name

2. Height

3. Alternate between male and female

4. Last two digits of their cell or home phone numbers

5. Length of hair

6. Color of clothes

7. Birth date (month and day only)

Alternate Version: (blindfolds are needed)
Stay in the same teams. The two teams should face each other again. The first person on the left side is blindfolded, followed by every other person in the line. Repeat several of the commands from "Quick Line Up." The first team to complete the command is the winner. The overall winner is the team that wins 2 out of 3 competitions. Afterward, blindfold those who were not the last time.

Debrief the activity with the following questions:

What did you learn about leadership through this team initiative?

Who emerged as leaders?

What skills were necessary to obey the commands as quickly as possible?

Why must a leader act decisively at the right moment?

Close this lesson with a prayer of protection for the hearts and minds of these young leaders. The world wages a constant battle to influence them in destructive ways-pray for God's protection so that they can continue to develop godly attitudes and noble character and lead from a pure heart.

Lesson Summary:
- Doing = **conduct and action**

- Being = **character and attitudes**

- Leadership is a combination of doing and being—**doing flows out of being**

Lesson One

Doing Flows out of Being

Introduction:
If you know who a leader is supposed to be (in terms of godly character), it's easier to determine what a leader is supposed to do. Doing flows out of being.

Going Public:
When was a time you tried acting a certain way that wasn't consistent with who you really are?

Getting Focused:
Read Psalm 78:72.

    1. Leaders are _____.

    2. Leaders have _____.

    3. Leaders have _____.

Growing Deeper:
Aim to be a person of character first; then your actions will naturally align with God's purposes.

Philippians 2:14

_____
_____
_____

39

LeaderTreks.

Colossians 1:10
_____
_____
_____

2 Timothy 2:15
_____
_____
_____

James 1:19-20
_____
_____
_____

1 Peter 1:15
_____
_____
_____

Lesson Summary:
- Doing = _____ _____
- Being = _____ _____
- Leadership is a combination of doing and being—_____
_____.

40

Lesson Two:

What are the Tasks of a Leader?

Introduction:
Leaders face a multitude of tasks, but five leadership tasks are essential. Together they serve as a map for all leaders to move toward success. Any project, goal or mission can be accomplished if leaders follow these five tasks.

In this lesson, students will:
- Examine the five tasks of a leader.
- Study Nehemiah's leadership in a challenging situation.
- Practice the five tasks of a leader in a real project.

Going Public:
Would other people say you are a "focused" or "unfocused" person most of the time?

Note: You're looking for the most honest answer possible. Challenge students to "go public" with their fears and emotions as they relay their own personal experiences.

Expert Opinions:
"The task of the leader is to get his people from where they are to where they have not been." *Henry Kissinger*

"The first responsibility of a leader is to define reality. The last is to say thank you. In between, the leader is a servant." *Max DePree*

"The task of a leader is to tune everyone into shared goals, to put everyone in their right places, to help everyone acquire confidence in their own abilities." *Vladimir Putin*

"The task of a leader is two-fold: to push us towards the rapids and away from the rocks." *Ron Cole*

"Be sure you know the condition of your flocks, give careful attention to your herds." *Proverbs 27:23*

Getting Focused:
To introduce this lesson to students, say something like:

Leaders can sometimes feel overwhelmed by their goals. They want to accomplish so much; it seems that they will never have enough time to do it all. However, a leader must focus on only five basic tasks in order to be successful in any under-taking. We're going to learn about those tasks by reading the story of an ultra marathon runner who made history.

Read the following true story to students. You may wish to google "Cliff Young" and show his picture, too.

Each year Australia hosts an endurance race from Sydney to Melbourne that attracts elite runners from around the world. The 500-mile race lasts five days and is considered to be the longest and toughest of all ultra marathons. Typically the competitor's strategy is to run 100 miles a day at a speed of 5.5 miles per hour for 18 hours straight and then sleep for 6 hours. In the 1983 inaugural race, an unknown potato farmer named Cliff Young showed up to compete without registering in advance. He immediately attracted media attention for some very good reasons.

Cliff was 61 years old while his competitors were between the ages of 18-20. The athletes had participated in endurance races for many years; Cliff's experience was limited to running after his brother's sheep. Prior to the race the media asked Cliff who he was and what he was doing. He told them, "I believe I can run this race, it's only two more days. Five days. I've run sheep for three." Most runners had corporate sponsorships; Cliff paid the fee himself. The 150 elite athletes were assisted by teams of coaches, trainers and dieticians; the only member of Cliff's support team was a trainer, his 81-year old mother. While the athletes gathered at the starting line wearing expensive, customized racing gear, Cliff wore overalls and galoshes over his work boots just as he wore every day in the field chasing sheep.

When the starting gun sounded, the competitors sprinted off; Cliff shuffled along in his galoshes at a brisk walk, not a run. After 18 hours, the athletes stopped for their 6 hours of sleep. Cliff kept going; in fact, he shuffled for five days straight without ever taking a break. By the last night, Cliff had passed the sleeping runners by a wide margin. He won first place beating the competition by 9 hours and instantly became a national hero. When Cliff Young finished the 500-mile race, the media asked him what he thought enabled him to win. He told them that he won because he didn't know he was supposed to sleep. In his mind, he was chasing sheep and trying to outrun a storm. Today the Sydney to Melbourne race is named in honor of Cliff Young. However, the greatest honor is that athletes now copy Cliff's unorthodox racing style.

Ask:
How does Cliff's story inspire you?
Why must a leader challenge the status quo?

Cliff took an unconventional road to success, but he did so using five essential leadership tasks. Together they serve as a map for all leaders toward success. Any project, goal or mission can be accomplished if leaders follow these five tasks:

1. Determine the scope and goals of the project.

2. Calculate the resources and people needed. Figure out how to best use the resources and people's gifts and abilities.

3. Cast the vision. Share with people what you plan to do and why.

4. Navigate the obstacles. Anticipate possible problems and solve those difficulties.

5. Evaluate the progress. Ask, "How can we do this better?"

Using the story of Cliff Young, challenge students to think through all five tasks.

1. **Determine** the scope and goals of the project.
One of the greatest challenges of being a leader is seeing the future. Leaders must be able to set the boundaries of a project and determine goals to ensure the project will be completed with excellence.

Ask: How did Cliff accomplish this task?
(Cliff Young knew that the race was 500 miles; his goal was to win the race. He understood what he needed to do to be successful.)

2. **Calculate** the people and resources needed to complete the project.
Leaders must put the right people in the right positions in order for a team to perform at maximum potential. Leaders must also provide the resources to complete projects, whether that includes money, materials or other necessities.

Ask: How did Cliff accomplish this task?
(In the 1983 ultra marathon Cliff Young's mother trained him using his everyday apparel

and footwear. These resources worked for him chasing sheep; Cliff and his mom figured these resources also would work for the race.)

3. <u>**Cast**</u> the vision.

A clearly communicated vision can change everything. If leaders are able to articulate the vision, no obstacle will stand in the way of their mission.

Ask: How did Cliff accomplish this task?
(Cliff envisioned running after sheep just two more days than he ordinarily had to do. He knew he could run the race and told others he planned to do so.)

4. <u>**Navigate**</u> the obstacles.

Leaders need to think about what is coming next and deal with problems before those issues sabotage a project. Leaders also need to deal with conflict.

Ask: How did Cliff accomplish this task?
(Cliff faced three basic obstacles: time, distance and energy. He determined to navigate the obstacles by shuffling non-stop in comfortable attire.)

5. <u>**Evaluate**</u> the performance.

Leaders need to ask, "How can we do this better?" Consistent, honest evaluation is the leader's tool to bring about growth in followers and to ensure excellence in all that his or her team does.

Ask: How did Cliff accomplish this task?
(When asked how he won, Cliff reviewed his strategy. He knew he would only do better than the others in the race if he did not sleep. So, he focused on chasing sheep throughout the night. Others evaluated his performance and adopted his unorthodox running style.)

Growing Deeper:

Let's take another look at one of Nehemiah's challenges while rebuilding the wall around Jerusalem-critics. Read the following passage from Nehemiah 4:1, 10-14 and identify principles, practices and personal qualities that made Nehemiah an effective leader:

> *1When Sanballat heard that we were rebuilding the wall, he became angry and was greatly incensed. He ridiculed the Jews ... 10Meanwhile, the people in Judah said, "The strength of the laborers is giving out, and there is so much rubble that we cannot rebuild the wall." 11Also our enemies said, "Before they know it or see us, we will be right there among them and will kill them and put an end to the work." ... 13Therefore I stationed some of the people behind the lowest points of the wall at the exposed places, posting them by families, with their swords, spears and bows. 14After I looked things over, I stood up and said to the nobles, the officials and the rest of the people, "Don't be afraid of them. Remember the Lord, who is great and awesome, and fight for your brothers, your sons and your daughters, your wives and your homes."*

Ask:
What were Nehemiah's challenges?
Why were the people discouraged?
How did Nehemiah demonstrate focus?
Why do you think he stationed them in families?

Listed below are suggested leadership principles from this passage about Nehemiah:

> Leaders have to <u>**focus**</u> on a plan.
>
> Leaders <u>**inspire**</u> full commitment from followers.
>
> Leaders <u>**prepare**</u> for the attacks of their enemies.
>
> Leaders <u>**encourage**</u> followers with the right words at the right times.

"What In the World Is It?" Activity

In this activity, students will begin practicing the five tasks of a leader.

Materials:

    glue, tape, balloons, glitter, pipe cleaners, boxes, bags, newspapers, construction paper and other items. Be creative!

Instructions

Divide students into teams of four to five people each. Give each team a variety of craft materials. Tell each team, "Your mission is to construct a product that has a specific purpose. Your product must have a function and it must work. Undertake this project by following the five tasks of a leader. After you complete the project, you will be asked for a sales pitch on the benefits of using your product. Try to get another team to 'buy' your product."

Give students 10-12 minutes to complete the project and an additional 5 minutes for their sales pitch.

The teams will listen to the sales pitches and make a decision on purchasing or not purchasing based on these criteria:

- Each team can only purchase one product, and it cannot be their own product.

- The product your team selects must actually work and serve the most useful function.

Note: Effective teams rotate these roles among the members. Be sure each role is represented in each team.

    - Leader: Guide the team's work

    - Scribe: Record the team's ideas

    - Encourager: Help the team persist

    - Reporter: Share results

Debrief the activity by asking:

How did you utilize the five tasks of a leader in this exercise:

    1. Determine scope and goals (What was your goal?)

    2. Calculate people and resources (What items did you have?)

    3. Cat the vision (sales pitch)

    4. Navigate the obstacles (team attitudes, time limits, etc.)

    5. Evaluate the performance (Did others purchase it? What would you change?)

Close by challenging students to continue thinking through the five tasks of a leader as they undertake daily activities like: completing a group homework assignment at school, preparing for their next sports competition, etc. Leaders develop these skills through using them repeatedly in ordinary situations. You may wish to ask students to share next week one situation they processed in the past week using one or more of these five skills.

Lesson Summary:

The Five Tasks of a Leader are:

- Determine scope and goals
- Calculate people and resources
- Cast the vision
- Navigate the obstacles
- Evaluate the performance

From The Student Guide

Lesson Two

What are the Tasks of a Leader?

Introduction:
Leaders face a multitude of tasks, but five leadership tasks are essential.

Going Public:
Would other people say you are a "focused" or "unfocused" person most of the time?

Getting Focused:
Any project, goal or mission can be accomplished if leaders follow these five tasks:

1. _____ the scope and goals of the project.

2. _____ the resources and people needed. Figure out how to best use the resources and people's gifts and abilities.

3. _____ the vision. Share with people what you plan to do and why.

4. _____ the obstacles. Leaders anticipate possible problems and solve those difficulties.

5. _____ the progress. Leaders need to ask, "How can we do this better?"

Growing Deeper:
Read Nehemiah 4:1, 10-14

41

- Leaders have to _____ on a plan.
- Leaders _____ full commitment from followers.
- Leaders _____ for the attacks of their enemies.
- Leaders _____ followers with the right words at the right times.

Activity:
1. _____
_____

2. _____
_____

3. _____
_____

4. _____
_____

5. _____
_____

Lesson Summary:
- Determine goals
- Calculate resources
- Cast vision
- Navigate obstacles
- Evaluate Progress

42

Lesson Three

Having a Mission

Introduction:
Leaders need to understand the definition, characteristics, and importance of their mission.

In this lesson, students will:

- Understand that a mission is a special assignment from God, one's unique purpose in life.

- Study three biblical examples of receiving and responding to a mission

- Realize a specific burden, passion and vision God could use for their personal mission.

Going Public:
What were you born to do?

Note: You're looking for the most honest answer possible. Challenge students to "go public" with their fears and emotions as they relay their own personal experiences.

Expert Opinion:

"Here's the test to find out whether your mission on earth is finished. If you're alive, it isn't." *Richard Bach*

"When you discover your mission, you will feel its demand. It will fill you with enthusiasm and a burning desire to get to work on it." *W. Clement Stone.*

"The place God calls you to is the place where your deep gladness and the world's deep hunger meet." *Frederick Buechner*

"When he had received the drink, Jesus said, "It is finished." With that, he bowed his head and gave up his spirit." *John 19:30 (TNIV)*

Getting Focused:
To introduce this lesson to students, say something like:

When you discover your mission in life, you will feel as though you were "born to do it." You were created for this specific purpose, but you weren't born knowing HOW to do it. That's why leadership must be learned over time so we know how to do what it feels as if we were born to do. Have a volunteer read the following quote by a prominent author on leadership:

"Knowing what God wants you to do in your life is like having a road map to a place you've never been before." *Pat Williams*

Ask:
Is it possible to know what God's mission is for your life? Why or why not?
How is God's plan like a roadmap?
Why is it somewhere you've never been before?

Say something like:
A mission is a special assignment from God-it is your unique purpose in life. To know that God chose you from the billions of other people on this earth to carry out a specific job for Him is an awesome discovery. He chose you because of how He uniquely made you. All of your experiences, skills and the whole of your personality uniquely equip you to do something that no one else can do.

Teach students the following key points about a mission:

1. A Mission = **a special assignment from God**

Ask:
Have you ever felt God's call to a particular mission or purpose?
How do you know if you are on the right mission?

2. You have a choice in your mission: **Accept it or Run from it**

Ask:
What fears are associated with accomplishing God's mission?
If you experience difficulties and persecution on your mission, does it mean you did not choose the right mission? Explain.

Say something like:
Accepting your mission doesn't mean you perform it perfectly. He allows us to be a part of His work despite and sometimes even because of our failures. The key is to commit to doing whatever it is wholeheartedly. He's calling you to discover your mission and to work alongside Him for His kingdom.

"Would You Rather?" Activity

This activity is a twist on a fun game that will communicate the idea of accepting or rejecting an assignment.

The youth pastor will pose two situations to a student who must answer which one he/she would "rather" do. Then the student must actually do whatever their choice is.

The rules are as follows:

1. You must choose one of the situations, even if you'd rather do neither!

2. You must do exactly what the assignment describes.

3. Each student gets one pass for the whole game. If he/she passes, the next student gets the same set of two questions.

4. Two people in a row cannot pass.

Note: Read the following assignments in pairs. You can mix and match the assignments as you wish. The first one is an example.

Would you rather...

Go to the front of the room and sing one verse from any song you sing in church.

　　　　OR

Tell the person next to you three things you like about their hair.

(student chooses and performs assignment)

Assignments include: (you can add more/less)

Answer any question the youth pastor asks you-truthfully!

- Stand up and *do 10 jumping jacks.*
- *Ask the person next to you to time you to see how long you can hold your breath.*
- *Write a two-line poem about your favorite ice cream flavor and recite it to the group.*
- *Make up a spontaneous cheer about your high school and perform it for the group.*
- *Give all of the change in your pockets right now to the person sitting next to you. If you don't have any change, lucky you. You have a free pass.*
- *Share with the group what the most played songs are in your ipod, cds, etc.*
- *Share with the group your top three favorite movies.*
- *Touch the tip of your nose with your tongue.*
- *Attempt to kiss your elbow. (note-this is impossible, but try anyway)*
- *Do your best impersonation of the youth pastor and try to get the group to guess who you're impersonating.*
- *Talk for one minute (without stopping) about what you ate at one of your meals yesterday...have a friend time you.*
- *Close your eyes. Stand on one foot. Hold your arms out beside you. Hold this pose for one minute without faltering. Repeatedly say, "I think I can. I think I can. I think I can," the whole time.*

Debrief this experience by asking the following questions about mission:

Why doesn't God force us to follow His plan for our lives?

Right now, are you closer to accepting or running from God's unique mission for your life? Why or why not?

Say something like:

Many of the stories in the Old and New Testaments are about people on a mission. God gives them a special assignment and we learn how they respond to the mission and what happens as a result. Let's look at several examples.

Growing Deeper:

Divide students into three groups. Assign each group one of the following examples and ask each group to identify the mission and response to the mission.

"As Jesus was walking beside the Sea of Galilee, he saw two brothers, Simon called Peter and his brother Andrew. They were casting a net into the lake, for they were fishermen. 'Come, follow me,' Jesus said, 'and I will make you fishers of men.' At once they left their nets and followed him." Matthew 4:18-20

Ask:

What was the mission?

    (To follow Jesus)

What was the response?

    (Peter and Andrew followed right away.)

"The word of the LORD came to Jonah son of Amittai: 'Go to the great city of Nineveh and preach against it, because its wickedness has come up before me.' But Jonah ran away from the LORD and headed for Tarshish. He went down to Joppa, where he found a ship bound for that port. After paying the fare, he went aboard and sailed for Tarshish to flee from the LORD." Jonah 1:1-3

Ask:
What was the mission?
(To go to Nineveh and preach against it.)

What was the response?
(Jonah ran away as far as he could!)

"On one occasion, while he was eating with them, he gave them this command: 'Do not leave Jerusalem, but wait for the gift my Father promised, which you have heard me speak about. For John baptized with water, but in a few days you will be baptized with the Holy Spirit.' Then they returned to Jerusalem from the hill called the Mount of Olives, a Sabbath day's walk from the city. When they arrived, they went upstairs to the room where they were staying ... They all joined together constantly in prayer, along with the women and Mary the mother of Jesus, and with his brothers. Acts 9:4-5, 12-14

Ask:
What was the mission?
(To stay in Jerusalem until they received the Holy Spirit.)

What was the response?
(The disciples obeyed Him and prayed.)

Say something like:
In the examples above, Peter and Andrew immediately obeyed. On the other hand, Jonah tried to run. He suffered severe consequences until finally he accepted God's mission. Even then God had to teach Him more about His compassion and grace. Finally, the remaining eleven disciples obeyed Jesus and went back to Jerusalem to wait for the Holy Spirit. The question is: What will you do when God gives you your mission?

Everyone's mission is different, but each mission has the same things in common:

1. <u>Mission comes with responsibility</u>. Since you are unique, you are the only one that can accomplish it. God has not called multiple people to that mission. He has called you. Therefore, you have a responsibility to accomplish it. No one else is as gifted at your mission as you are. Your faithfulness following God will open up other doors and give you more responsibility.

2. <u>Disobeying the mission brings severe consequences</u>. As you saw with Jonah, turning to run will make you miserable. It states in Romans 11:29 that God's gifts and His call are irrevocable. You cannot send it back or ask for another mission. Running away is not an option either. Sometimes your mission may change over time as you learn more and grow, but you never "retire" from your mission.

3. <u>Mission demands action</u>. Your mission is not something that is waiting for your college graduation; it is time to start now. God called David as a boy and he took on a giant. He's calling you to something great, not because you're so great, but because He is! He has called you because He knows you can do it. Don't let your flaws, failures or doubts get in the way. With God working in you, there is nothing you can't accomplish. Your role will be to develop your faith in God and move into action.

How do you discover your mission? The way you discover your mission in life can be expressed this way:

Burden + Passion + Vision = Mission

Note: this formula is very important to communicate to students.

God doesn't use a step-by-step formula to reveal His assignment. He wants us to pray and listen. Your mission is a combination of something that burdens your heart, something you are passionate about and something you have a vision to accomplish. As you combine these three ideas, your God-given mission starts to emerge.

Ask students to spend the next 15 minutes alone in an area in the room where they can focus on the following questions. Provide pen and paper.

- What burdens your heart?

- What is your passion in life?

- What is the unique vision God has given you to help others?

- What are your unique abilities and spiritual gifts?

- What are some key words, ideas or themes that seem related throughout this equation? In what ways do these areas intersect or overlap?

Fill in the blank:

- I believe God may be calling me to do:_____

Note: Although this is not a formal mission-statement exercise, some students may be challenged to go ahead and begin writing a personal mission statement. At the least, have students get together with one other person at the conclusion of their individual time and share their current understanding what God may be calling them to do. It may be a raw and broad idea at this stage.

Close by challenging students to pray for each other about God's leading for the next week until you meet again.

Lesson Summary:

- A mission is a special assignment from God, your **unique** purpose in life.

- There are many biblical **examples** of mission.

- Leaders **find**, **follow**, and fulfill their **mission**.

- Mission incudes responsibility and **demands** action.

Lesson Three

Having a Mission

Introduction:
Leaders need to understand the definition, characteristics, and importance of their mission.

Going Public:
What were you born to do?

Getting Focused:

1. A Mission = _____ _____

2. You have a choice in your mission: _____
_____

Growing Deeper:
Matthew 4:18-20
_____
_____

Jonah 1:1-3
_____
_____

Acts 9:4-5,12-14
_____
_____

43

---

3 Aspects of Mission

1. _____

2. _____

3. _____

B u r d e n + P a s s i o n + V i s i o n = M i s s i o n

• What burdens your heart?

• What is your passion in life?

• What is the unique vision God has given you to help others?

• What are your unique abilities and spiritual gifts?

• What are some key words, ideas or themes that seem related throughout this equation? In what ways do these areas intersect or overlap?

Fill in the blank:
I believe God may be calling me to:_____
_____
_____

Lesson Summary:

• A mission is a special assignment from God, your _____ purpose in life.

• There are many biblical _____ of mission.

• Leaders _____, _____, and _____ their mission.

• Mission includes responsibility and _____ action.

44

Lesson Four

Leading by Example

Introduction:
Leaders must know how to lead by example. Words are powerful, but leaders must back up their words by showing others the way.

In this lesson, students will:
- Reflect on what it does and does not mean to lead through example.
- Study biblical principles in Philippians 2 for leading through example.
- Consider their own personal example and its impact on their leadership

Going Public:
What would the world's perception of Christianity be if every Christian were just like me?

Note: You're looking for the most honest answer possible. Challenge students to "go public" with their fears and emotions as they relay their own personal experiences.

Expert Opinions:
"A leader leads by example, whether he intends to or not." *Unknown*

"Setting an example is not the main means of influencing another, it is the only means." *Albert Einstein*

"Preach the Gospel at all times and when necessary use words." *St. Francis of Assisi*

"Your walk talks and your talk talks; but your walk talks more than your talk talks." *Unknown*

"Follow my example, as I follow the example of Christ." *1 Corinthians 11:1*

Getting Focused:
To introduce this lesson to students, say something like:

What does it mean to lead by example? We are always leading by example-people watch our lives every day to see what we are about. However, what example or impression do we leave with them? And what does it say about our values, goals and commitments?

Ask:
Who is the best living example of what it means to be a Christian leader?

Have students share their answers. Next, consider the following two examples. Ask for volunteers to read the stories.

Story #1

Note: The following story is fictitious but instructive.

A General addressed his troops before sending them into battle. As he stood before them in the wee hours of the morning, he began his speech, "I send you now into an uncertain future. No one can say whether you will succeed or fail, live or die. But whatever befalls you, I can assure you that you have my undying gratitude for your sacrifice." The General walked among his troops as he spoke, a look of grave concern on his face. They were already exhausted from several days' travel, but each man stood ready for battle, weapon in hand.

The General suddenly stopped, turned to the troops and with a strange look of relief on his face said, "I will remain here at headquarters, because someone must take care of business. But I will think of you often and pray for you constantly." The soldiers were stunned! However, before any of the commanding officers could speak, the General turned on his heel, waved his hand over his shoulder and said, "Good luck." He then disappeared into his tent.

Ask:
Imagine that you are one of the troops listening to this address. What thoughts would be going through your mind as you listened to the General's speech?
Which words in the speech would inspire you? Which parts might anger you?

Say something like:
People follow leaders who set an example. A tribal chief told a group of African missionaries that he respected them because "you have eaten the same dust we have." He meant that the believers lived as the Africans did, suffering the same hardships. Their example allowed them to share the Gospel with villagers. Many became Christians as a result.

Story #2

Note: This is a true story from Angola, Africa.

Three college students went to Uganda, Africa as part of a film project for one of their classes. They were shocked to discover that thousands of children were fleeing their homes each night to avoid abduction. A rebel force fighting against the government was kidnapping young people to become child soldiers in its army. Children ages 3 to 17 left their homes in the middle of the night in an exodus called "night commuters." They walked throughout the night to get to safe shelters that were up to 12 miles away.

The filmmakers, Jason Russell, Bobby Bailey and Lauren Russell started a nonprofit organization called "Invisible Children, Inc." The organization's purpose was to raise awareness of this issue in the United States. The founders hoped to attract other young people to join their cause and pressure the government to take action against it. They toured the country holding public viewings of the film they made called Invisible Children.

Their example of taking action to solve a problem gained worldwide support. In April 2006 the group held a rally that attracted 80,000 young people from many nations.

They held protest marches in 130 major cities, spending the night in city parks in a show of support for Ugandan children. Their campaign slogan "To make a difference; to end a war" is having some effect. The situation in Uganda is improving thanks to the heroic efforts and example of three college students.

Ask:
What makes this story unusual?
How are those three college students leading through example?
Why do you think the protest marches were so successful?

Leading by example involves the following principles:

1. Be an example of what you want others to <u>become</u>. The Indian civil rights leader Mahatma Gandhi once said, "We must become the change we want to see." Leaders demonstrate firsthand who their followers must be and what it is they must do. Unlike the General in the example above, they don't send others off to fight their battles. They stand shoulder to shoulder with their people in doing the work. You will never take people further than you yourself are willing to go. Since we want people to become like Christ, they must see Christ in us. As the Apostle Paul proclaimed, "Follow my example, as I follow the example of Christ."

2. Be an example of <u>depending</u> on His strength, not human effort. Leaders know that there is a limit to human strength, but God's power is unlimited. Christians cannot live a supernatural life apart from supernatural power. Leaders learn to depend on the power of the Holy Spirit to provide all the resources needed to accomplish God's work. Galatians 3:3 says, "Are you so foolish? After beginning with the Spirit, are you now trying to attain your goal by human effort?"

3. Be an example of <u>inspiration</u>. Leaders speak in a way that inspires and motivates their followers. But they avoid saying things that are untrue or unfeeling. They follow the Apostle Paul's counsel to "speak the truth in love." Truthful, genuine inspiration results in a genuine response from those around us.

4. Be an example of a <u>promise</u> kept. Leaders do what they say they will do. Leaders who fail to fulfill their promises soon find that no one is following them. People are drawn to leaders who follow through on their promises. Jesus told us, "Simply let your 'Yes' be 'Yes,' and your 'No' be 'No'."

5. Be an example of <u>confession</u> and <u>forgiveness</u>. Leaders admit their mistakes and seek forgiveness as necessary. There is something powerful about a leader who says, "I'm sorry. I was wrong. Please forgive me." It reminds everyone that the leader is human. There is no such thing as a perfect leader. Every leader will eventually disappoint. However, a leader who demonstrates humility is a leader worth following. James 4:6 reminds us, "God opposes the proud but gives grace to the humble."

Growing Deeper:
Read Philippians 2:5-11 and identify ways that believers can follow the example of Jesus Christ.

"5Your attitude should be the same as that of Christ Jesus: 6Who, being in very nature God, did not consider equality with God something to be grasped, 7but made himself nothing, taking the very nature of a servant, being made in human likeness. 8And being found in appearance as a man, he humbled himself and became obeddient to death—even death on a cross! 9Therefore God exalted Him to the highest place and gave Him the name that is above every name, 10that at the name of Jesus every knee should bow, in heaven and on earth and under the earth, 11and every tongue confess that Jesus Christ is Lord, to the glory of God the Father."

Ask:
According to this passage, what principles can we learn from Christ's example? (name at least 3-4 elements)
Does it ever bother you that the biblical example to follow is a servant, not a superstar? Be honest and explain.

Is it possible to follow Christ's example perfectly? Why or why not?

Possible principles related to Christ's example include:

    1. He was **<u>obedient</u>**

    2. He was completely **<u>humble</u>**

    3. He was a **<u>servant</u>** to others

    4. He did not put the focus on **<u>Himself</u>**, but on God

5. His **example** led to a glorious reward

Say something like:
We need to spend some time focusing on the example we give to others. Being an example makes one vulnerable because people are always watching you. You live your life on display for others to see the good (because you are a Christian) and the bad (because you are still human). If other people look to you for an example of a Christian leader, what do they see in you?

"Do You See What I See?" Activity

This initiative will provide valuable self-analysis for each participant and help them become more effective leaders. This is an extremely powerful initiative. When you begin the activity, be sure that all participants take it seriously. It will work better if partners are of the same gender.

Rules:

1. Pair up with someone who does not know you very well.

2. Stand up and face your partner as close as possible without either partner feeling uncomfortable.

3. Maintain absolute silence during the initiative unless otherwise permitted.

4. Look at your partner carefully. Notice what you see. Go beyond physical features such as the color of the person's eyes. Instead look intently into your partner's eyes while you focus on the following questions:

   - What positive and negative character qualities do you think they perceive in you?

   - What emotions do you think they see within you?

   - What strengths and weakness do you think they detect about you?

   - What symbol or image about yourself comes up inside you right now? For example, Jesus called Peter a rock. What metaphor is triggered in your mind as you imagine your partner searching beyond your eyes?

When instructed, you will sit down and debrief the activity together by sharing your findings about yourself. Be specific. Be truthful. Sit facing your partner. Either person may go first, but that individual should continue without interruption. No questions or comments may be made by the person listening to the report. When finished, the person listening should thank the reporter for his or her insights.

Now switch roles and allow the other partner to report. Follow the same rules as before until the report has been completed. Once again, the listener thanks the reporter for his or her insights.

Debrief as follows in the large group:

- How hard was this activity for you?

- What made it difficult?

- How accurate do you think your partner's perception of himself/herself is?

- What's the difference between what we WANT others to see in us and what we really are?

- How can you change your example to improve your leadership effectiveness?

Lesson Summary:

- Leaders demonstrate **Christ-likeness**.

- Leaders depend on the power of the **Holy Spirit** to be a good example.

- Leaders are not **perfect** examples.

- Leaders do what they **promise**.

- Leaders display **humility**.

Leadership365

Lesson Four

Leading by Example

Introduction:

Leaders must know how to lead by example. Words are powerful, but leaders must back up their words by showing others the way.

Going Public:

What would the world's perception of Christianity be if every Christian were just like me?

Getting Focused:

1. Be an example of what you want others to _____.
2. Be an example of _____ on His strength, not human effort.
3. Be an example of _____.
4. Be an example of a _____ kept.
5. Be an example of _____ and _____.

Growing Deeper:

Philippians 2:5-11

1. He was _____
2. He was completely _____
3. He was a _____ to others
4. He did not put the focus on _____, but on God
5. His _____ led to a glorious reward

45

46

LeaderTreks

Lesson Summary:

Leaders demonstrate _____.

Leaders depend on the power of the _____ to be a good example.

Leaders are not _____ examples.

Leaders do what they _____.

Leaders display _____.

Lesson Five

Leading through Teams

Introduction:

Leaders must know how to lead through teams. Others utilize our strengths and compensate for our weaknesses. We learn and grow by watching others around us. We are motivated to do more than we could on our own, and teams make those goals possible! Ultimately, being on a team makes its members better people.

In this lesson, students will:

- Examine the factors the make a great team.

- Study the biblical example of Ruth and Naomi.

- Determine that they will lead most effectively through a team.

Going Public:

Do you want to do something great with your life?

Note: You're looking for the most honest answer possible. Challenge students to "go public" with their fears and emotions as they relay their own personal experiences.

Expert Opinions:

"Individual commitment to a group effort -- that is what makes a team work, a company work, a society work, a civilization work." *Vince Lombardi*

"After this the Lord chose seventy others. He sent them out two together to every city and place where He would be going later." *Luke 10:1 (NLV)*

Getting Focused

To introduce this lesson to students, say something like:

It's part of human nature to want to do something great. However, our potential to do something great is at its highest level when we choose to work with a team, not on our own. When we are on a team we feel a sense of belonging and we gain confidence knowing that there are no limits to what we can achieve working together.

Solicit two volunteers to read one quotation each and explain what it means.

Ask:
Is this statement true? Why or why not?

"The speed of the leader is the speed of the team." Unknown

"No man will make a great leader who wants to do it all himself, or to get all the credit for doing it." Andrew Carnegie, philanthropist

"My job is to lead the team to where we want to go. In order for that to happen, we all have to be on the same page." Donovan McNabb, athlete

Optional Activity

In a previous lesson in Semester One (Why Study Leadership?), you learned the acronym for TEAM: Together Everyone Achieves More. Can you think of another acronym that communicates as well? Be creative!

Finish the acronym:

T -

E -

A -

M -

Accept any acronym that works.

Say something like:
It's important for us to think about the nature and importance of teams because God has assigned us to do His work in conjunction with others. Adam had Eve. Moses had Aaron. Jesus had the disciples. The disciples had each other once Jesus returned to heaven. What are some other popular and/or powerful examples of teams that come to your mind?

Get students together in teams of three people each to list examples of great teams in each of the following categories:

- Sports
- Politics
- History
- Entertainment
- Your church
- Your school

Now pick one example from your list above and discuss, "What makes this team a great team?" List at least five reasons.

1.

2.

3.

4.

5.

Share the following illustration about the power of synergy:

A farmer went out to plow his field with two horses named Dunhurst and Barlycorn. Dunhurst was an older horse with much experience in pulling a plow. He was a disciplined and dependable animal. Barlycorn, on the other hand, was a younger horse with little experience in the field. He was full of energy and very independent.

Most days the two horses worked together and the farmer accomplished a great deal. On a few days the two horses had two different minds. One pulled one way and the second horse pulled in a different direction. Those were tough days for the farmer. Not only did he work harder, but by the end of the day he plowed far less of the field.

Researchers measured the power of one horse working alone. They did the same thing with a second horse. They discovered that the power generated by two horses working together was 5 times the strength of either horse working alone. "Synergy" is the name given to the extra power generated by teamwork. It is a scientific principle that the combined effect of two working together is greater than the individual contribution. When a team works together it always accomplishes more.

Ask:
What do successful teams have in common?

Suggested factors could include:

Chemistry

Common goals

Skill level

Harmony

Strong leadership

Hard work

Self-sacrifice

Perseverance

Say something like:
Building a strong team requires personal relationships and commitment. When life is easy, we have no problem staying committed. It's when life becomes hard and we face challenges that our commitment is tested. Commitment to the team goes far beyond what is comfortable and safe. It is through commitment that an individual shows his or her strength. Consider the story of a great biblical team, Ruth and Naomi.

Growing Deeper:

Note: This Bible study focuses on Ruth and Naomi-please review the story prior to the meeting and make special note of what you learn about teamwork. The context of the story is Ruth's commitment to Naomi and her willingness to sacrifice her own needs and desires to support her mother-in-law. From this perspective, their story teaches great truths about teamwork.

Have students read selected verses from Ruth 1: 7-11, 14-18.

"7With her two daughters-in-law she left the place where she had been living and set out on the road that would take them back to the land of Judah. 8Then Naomi said to her two daughters-in-law, 'Go back, each of you, to your mother's home. May the Lord show kindness to you, as you have shown to me. 9May the Lord grant that each of you will find rest in the home of another husband.' Then she kissed them and they wept aloud 10and said to her, 'we will go back with you to your people.' 11But Naomi said, 'Return home, my daughters. Why would you come with me? Am I going to have any more sons, who could become your husbands?'...14At this time they wept again. Then Orpah kissed her mother-in-law good-bye, but Ruth clung to her. 15'Look,' said Naomi, 'your sister-in-law is going back to her people and her gods. Go back with her.' 16But Ruth replied, 'Don't urge me to leave you. Where you go I will go, and where you stay I wil stay. Your people will be my people and your God my God. 17Where you die I will die, and there will I be buried. May the Lord deal with me, be it ever so severely, if anything but death separates you and me'. 18 When Naomi realized that Ruth was determined to go with her, she stopped urging her."

Instruct students to think about Ruth's situation as she contemplated whether to stay or go. Complete the sentence below regarding Ruth's steadfast commitment to stay with Naomi despite some specific challenges.

Ruth was committed to Naomi despite ...

Examples include:

> Ruth was committed to Naomi despite
>
>> ...Her husband's death
>>
>> ...leaving Moab
>>
>> ...leaving her family
>>
>> ...crying openly
>>
>> ...her friend Oprah's departure
>>
>> ...all Naomi's pleas to leave her
>>
>> ...rejecting her own people and gods
>>
>> ...the possibility of her own death if she didn't make the journey

Ruth insisted on staying beside Naomi instead of going alone. God honored her commitment to team. He positioned her to become part of Jesus' lineage through her subsequent marriage to Boaz. As it turns out, God had a purpose in Ruth's connection to Naomi, but He left the choice up to Ruth as to whether or not to stay with her.

We may not know all the personal reasons why Ruth stayed, but everyone experiences similar emotions and benefits whenever they choose to be a part of a team.

Ask:
What are some of the reasons why people prefer being on a team instead of being alone?
What benefits are there to being on a team?

Possible answers include:

>   People want to be on a team that is doing something great.

>   Being on a team provides a sense of belonging.

>   Being on a team allows us to use our strengths.

>   Being on a team increases our motivation and personal growth.

>   Being on a team makes its members better people.

"Acme Rubber Band Company Challenge" Activity
This game was adapted from Tom Heck at teachmeteamwork.com

Very rarely will a group actually solve this challenge. It's that difficult. It will force the group to engage in dialogue and creative problem solving. Because the group will likely experience failure, it will provide them with a chance to determine what failure means to them.

Equipment:

Bucket

Single length of rope (size varies)

Single length of string (size varies)

Two large circles of elastic (large enough for a team to stretch)

Instructions

Form two teams and select two captains who will set up the equipment. The rope forms the larger circle. The string forms the inner circle. The bucket is in the middle of the inner circle. The goal is to form a circle, stretch a piece of elastic and attempt to release the stretched elastic into a bucket in the center of a circle. Share the following scenario with students:

The Acme Rubber Band Company has noticed how well your team is working together. They would like you to test the elasticity of their biggest rubber band. You must work as a team to stretch this rubber band to its limits and see if you can simultaneously release it to make it land within the target zone. The executives at Acme are relying on you.

Ground Rules:

>   A boundary circle will be marked out on the ground with a rope.

>   A string circle will be placed in the center of the boundary circle.

>   All team members must be spaced evenly outside and around the boundary circle.

>   The team will be given one elastic circle.

>   Each team member holds onto the elastic with two fingers.

>   The team backs up so the elastic is stretched out in a big circle.

>   The group must keep the elastic fully stretched just before the release.

>   The group must release the elastic simultaneously and in such a way that the elastic falls into the string circle.

The bucket must stay in the center of the circle.

The elastic must land inside the bucket through the simultaneous release by the team (example: the elastic cannot be thrown in to the bucket by one person).

After students have tried (most likely unsuccessfully) to complete the initiative, introduce a second version. Repeat the initiative, but make the outer and inner circle smaller and smaller. The team that accomplishes the goal in the smallest circle is the winner.

Debrief by asking the following questions:

What made this activity hard?
How important was it that everyone worked together?
What did this activity teach you about teamwork?

Prayer for Strong Team Commitment

Close this lesson by an intentional time of prayer regarding your team's commitment to each other. Like Ruth, life tests our commitment to each other. All of the students on your team will benefit from the team's reaffirmation of commitment to each other and to whatever it is God has called them to do.

Lesson Summary:

- Together, Everyone Achieves More

- Difficulties test our commitment to team

- God designed us to work best in teams

From The Student Guide

Lesson Five

Leading through Teams

Introduction:
We are motivated to do more than we could on our own, and teams make those goals possible!

Going Public:
Do you want to do something great with your life?

Getting Focused:
Examples of great teams:

_____
_____
_____
_____

What makes this team a great team?

1. _____
2. _____
3. _____
4. _____
5. _____

47

Successful teams have the following in common:

- Chemistry
- Common goals
- Skill level
- Harmony
- Strong leadership
- Hard work
- Self-sacrifice
- Perseverance

Growing Deeper:
Read Ruth 1: 7-11, 14-18.

Lesson Summary:
- Together Everyone Achieves More
- Difficulties test our commitment to team
- God designed us to work best in teams

48

Lesson Six

Practicing Team Focus

Introduction:
Leaders understand that teams need to focus in order to reach their potential. This is one discipline that separates average teams from great teams. Teams that are truly effective are those that can maintain a single-minded focus on the task at hand.

In this lesson, students will:
- Consider three key principles in creating team focus.
- Study the example of team focus in the lives of the Philippians believers.
- Understand the power of focus in successful teams

Going Public:
How would you characterize this team's potential?

Note: You're looking for the most honest answer possible. Challenge students to "go public" with their fears and emotions as they relay their own personal experiences.

Expert Opinions:
"Teams share the burden and divide the grief." *Doug Smith*

"Wearing the same shirts doesn't make you a team." *Buchholz and Roth*

"Coming together is a beginning. Keeping together is progress. Working together is success." *Henry Ford*

"Teams work better-when they work together." *Alice Vernon*

"So let's keep focused on that goal, those of us who want everything God has for us. If any of you have something else in mind, something less than total commitment, God will clear your blurred vision-you'll see it yet! Now that we're on the right track, let's stay on it." *Philippians 3:1*

Getting Focused:
To introduce this lesson to students, say something like:

Most teams struggle to focus at the very time they need to do so the most. When focus suffers, team performance decreases rapidly. An easy way to increase the level of your team performance is to focus during those key times. This is often easier said than done! We are going to look at the key requirements for team focus. This will help you start to unlock this powerful tool.

Share the following illustration:

The Flying Tigers was the nickname for three squadrons of fighter pilots operating in China and Burma during World War II. They had only 20 airplanes, but they painted a tough exterior on the nose with a shark-face emblem. This relatively small unit shot down 217 enemy planes in 31 combat missions. During this time period, The Flying Tigers lost 6 pilots and 16 aircraft.

The fighter group's success was the result of a strategy called concentration. The pilots always flew in pairs fully committed to the protection of their partners. Each pair focused their attack on one enemy aircraft. Consequently, in any dogfight the enemy was outnumbered 2 to 1 regardless of the total number of fighters in the battle.

The enemy never discovered the secret behind their principle of concentration. Yet the power of team focus was a key factor in The Flying Tigers winning the air battle over Southeast Asia.

Ask:
Why were The Flying Tigers so successful?
Why do you suppose the enemy never figured out the strategy?
How would you define what it means for a team to focus?
Who is someone you know who is really focused?
How does their presence affect the teams they are a part of?

Optional Activity
Video Clip: A Bug's Life, 1998, Disney/Pixar

Clip: "Around the Leaf?"

The clip takes place in the very beginning of the movie (about one minute). Some ants are traveling in a line when a leaf falls down and blocks their path. The ants go into a panic until one ant, clearly a leader in the group, says that they can just go around the leaf.

Say something like:
Sometimes teams lose focus so easily. They meet a challenge or run into something unanticipated, and it throws them off course. However, leaders help come up with solutions that help maintain focus during a "crisis." Let's watch this clip to see this point illustrated.

SHOW CLIP HERE

Key Lines:

FIRST BUG IN LINE: I'm lost!!! Where's the line?! What do we do?!

ANOTHER BUG: We'll be stuck here forever!

MR. SOIL: Do not panic! Do not panic! We are trained professionals. Now, stay calm. We are going around the leaf.

FIRST BUG: Around the leaf? I don't think we can do that.

MR. SOIL: Oh, nonsense! This is nothing compared to the "Twig of '93". (He begins to guide them around the fallen leaf.) That's it... that's it...good! There you go, there you go! Watch my eyes; don't look away. And here's the line again!

FIRST BUG: Thank you! Thank you, Mr. Soil!

MR. BUG: Good job, everybody!

Stop here at approximately 0:01:37.

Say something like:

Let's take a look at three basic components of team focus:

1. Team Focus Requires Individual Focus

It takes the focus of every individual to create team focus. A focused team is made of individuals who share the value of remaining focused. In other words, focus is not a job for just one person. Everyone on the team must be willing to keep each other focused.

Paul addressed this need in the lives of the Philippians by saying, "If you have any encouragement from being united with Christ, if any comfort from his love, if any fellowship with the Spirit, if any tenderness and compassion, then make my joy complete by being like-minded, having the same love, being one in spirit and purpose." Philippians 2:1-2. He wanted to see a group of believers who made their team stronger by each member being committed to the focus of their team. The world can change when a team maintains their commitment to individual focus.

2. Team Focus Requires Team Roles

Everyone on the team has a vital role to play. In 1 Corinthians 12, Paul describes the church as a body of intricate and interdependent parts: "Just as a body, though one, has many parts, but all its parts form one body, so it is with Christ" (verse 12). We each have a vital role to play.

Although you have a role in the Body of Christ, you don't choose your role. It was a gift to God for you to use and to make the rest of the Body stronger. Just like each part of your body was designed from birth for a specific purpose, so you were designed for a specific purpose within the Body of Christ. Your role in the Body of Christ is vital. If you don't do it, it won't get done. If you choose not to exercise your gift the entire Body of Christ will suffer. Your gift comes with the responsibility to use it to benefit the church.

3. Team Focus Requires Commitment to the Mission

The mission is what focuses and strengthens a group of individuals into a team. Sharing a common mission is essential to a team. A team that has no mission is in danger of falling apart. The slightest mistake or challenge will cause confusion and discouragement-the team may even disband. When a team shares a common mission, all members will work together to accomplish the goal. The most important question any team can ask is, "What is our mission? Why do we exist?"

"Egg No-Toss" Activity

As this game illustrates, our moments of highest performance only come when we are willing to focus on the task at hand.

Equipment

Adventure Hardware tubes (purchase from www.adventurehardware.com)

Marble or other ball

2 buckets

Instructions

Using the Adventure Hardware tubes your team must move the marble, ping pong ball or plastic "egg" from the starting point (a bucket full of eggs) to the finishing point of the pre-determined course (an empty bucket). The facilitator should set up a route/course to follow. The course will vary in length depending on size and ability of the team. The course should be long enough that team members have to spread out.

Explain the following scenario:

An egg is about to fall out of a bird's nest! Being the bird watcher that you are, you do not want anything to happen to the egg so you quickly gather your friends to help you transport the egg to safety. To ensure that no one touches the egg, you have provided tubes to transport the egg. You also ask that while the egg is in one of your friends' tubes that they not move their feet (as it will compromise the safety of the egg).

Rules:

- All team members must be used to complete the initiative.

- Each team member can only use one tube.

- The ball must begin at the starting bucket.

- When the ball is on a tube, the individual holding it cannot move his or her feet.

- Once "start" or "go" has been called, the ball cannot be touched by the individual (hands, face, etc).

- The team must follow the route or course the facilitator has set up.

- If the ball is dropped, it is brought back to the starting line and the team must start over.

- The team finishes when the last person drops the ball in the canister at the finish bucket.

Debrief this initiative using the questions below:

What was most frustrating for you in this game?
When were the times that your team was the most focused during this game?
When did they struggle with focusing?
How could you improve your performance next time?

Growing Deeper:
Read Philippians 2:1-2 (CEV provided below) and look for spiritual principles related to team focus.

"Christ encourages you, and his love comforts you. God's Spirit unites you, and you are concerned for others. Now make me completely happy! Live in harmony by showing love for each other. Be united in what you think, as if you were only one person."

Ask:
What role does the Holy Spirit play in a team?
What commands are in this passage?
What does it mean for several people on a team to think as one?

Listed below are suggested principles to make sure your team has discussed:

We become part of the "team in Christ" through the Holy Spirit.

One indicator of a "team" is harmony and unity.

A team thinks as one person when it is united in its values and goals.

Optional Activity

Encourage students to use an internet search engine for videos (e.g., Google, Yahoo, AOL, etc.). Type in the words "magnifying glass fire." Identify a clip that shows a magnifying glass being used to ignite a fire on some paper or brush. (Warn students: Do not do this experiment on your own!) Next week, ask a student to describe what he/she saw take place and explain how this illustration relates to the principle of team focus.

Close this session by challenging students to create a team symbol for focus. This may be a hand gesture or symbol (pointing to eyes, pointing upward, etc.) that will help remind them to come together when things get distracting (during a team meeting, for example). It will be a silent symbol to team members to remember they are there for a purpose.

Close with a time of prayer asking God to sharpen the team's focus over the next few weeks.

Lesson Summary:

- Team focus is a group of people concentrating on the task at hand.

- It takes the focus of every individual to create team focus.

- Everyone on a team has a vital role to play.

- The mission focuses and strengthens a group of individuals into a team.

From The Student Guide

Lesson Six

Practicing Team Focus

Introduction:
Leaders understand that teams need to focus in order to reach their potential.

Going Public:
How would you characterize this team's potential?

Getting Focused:
1. _____ team member must focus to create team focus.

2. Every team member has a _____ role to play on the team.

3. Every group of individuals becomes a team by focusing on the _____.

Growing Deeper:
Read Philippians 2:1-2.

We become part of the "team in Christ" through the Holy Spirit.

One indicator of a "team" is harmony and unity.

A team thinks as one person when it is united in its values and goals.

Lesson Summary:
- Team focus is a group of people concentrating on the task at hand.
- It takes the focus of every individual to create team focus.
- Everyone on a team has a vital role to play.
- The mission focuses and strengthens a group of individuals into a team.

Lesson Seven

Increasing Team Care

Introduction:

Leaders understand that great teams care deeply about each other. To this day, people are won to Christ most readily when a Christian takes the time to care for them. As Christ-followers we need to care for each person on our team. In fact, the measure of our team care becomes the way others see Christ through our team.

In this lesson, students will:

- Reflect on the meaning of team care

- Consider three key principles in creating team focus.

- Study the example of team focus in the lives of Barnabas and Paul.

Going Public:

Do you think this team as a whole truly cares about each other? Why or why not?

Note: You're looking for the most honest answer possible. Challenge students to "go public" with their fears and emotions as they relay their own personal experiences.

Expert Opinions:

"It is amazing how much you can accomplish when it doesn't matter who gets the credit." *Sandra Swinney*

"Teamwork: Simply stated, it is less me and more we." *Unknown*

"Definition of a great teammate: a person who makes their teammates look GREAT!" *Emily Kohlbus*

"The basic building block of good team building is for a leader to promote the feeling that every human being is unique and adds value." *Unknown*

"This is how everyone will recognize that you are my disciples-when they see the love you have for each other." *John 13:35 (The Message)*

Getting Focused:

To introduce this lesson to students, write the following quotation on a large piece of paper and place it prominently in the room:

"None of us is as smart as all of us"
-Ken Blanchard, author

Ask students to discuss the meaning of this quote and whether they agree or disagree.

Say something like:
If a team is going to practice team care, then they all must commit to caring for every individual. This means that every person is valued for who they are-a team member-and not simply for what they bring to the team. Our value in God and before each other is not dependent on what we can do, but on who we are in Christ. It is normal to connect with some people more than others. That's not what we are talking about. Even if you don't readily connect with someone, you still need to care about them. When the team stops caring for individuals, team-building stops.

Challenge students to consider how well they practice this principle. It's Christianity 101-but are they really doing it on a daily basis?

Ask students to answer silently:
Is there someone on the team that you have a hard time caring for?
Are you caring for others on this team on a daily basis?

Jesus placed a high value on love and care for the people on His team. He knew that a team that cared about each other was capable of much more than a team that had no concern for their fellow members. He worked hard to pass this value on to His disciples. The following principles show what Team Care really means:

1. Team Care Requires Direct **Communication**

One important way that we can show others on our team that we care about them is to communicate effectively with them. It takes time and energy to communicate and this demonstrates a caring heart to others on the team. Jesus provided His team an example of how to behave and then explained it to them so they could understand. Every team needs to grow in their level of team care by talking and communicating with one another. Jesus talked one-on-one with His team for three years and made them closely observe what He was trying to teach them before they were ready to accept their assignment. Often, like the night He washed their feet, they didn't "get" what he taught them until He demonstrated it.

2. Team Care Shows Value for the **Individual**

Jesus demonstrated a deep regard for each of His disciples, including Judas. He included Judas, even on the night he washed the disciples' feet, to show that we have no excuse not to care for every member of our team. Judas would betray Jesus to a horrible, painful death in just a few hours. Jesus, however, knew the value of each person on His team and chose to serve Judas anyway. We don't have a choice. We must care for each individual on our team.

3. Team Care Requires **Sacrifice**

Team care is measured by the amount of sacrifice team members are willing to make for each other. Without sacrifice, a team will never be able to reach its potential. Sacrifice is easy to talk about in theory but hard to do. In order to sacrifice, we must be willing to take less than we deserve, serve others around us and give more than we think we can.

Jesus continually sacrificed for His team. To us, sacrifice usually has limits. However, Jesus showed us limitless sacrifice in the way He loved His team, the disciples. His love for all of us eventually led to Him to the cross.

Say something like:
Think about what you can do to grow closer as a team. (Solicit some ideas from students.)

Continue to value each other and there will be no stopping you. We see this principle at work in Paul's life when he joined an already established team of disciples/followers after his dramatic conversion to Christianity. If team care had not been in place, there would be no room for Paul. As a result, the early church and the entire movement itself would have suffered.

Growing Deeper:

Read Acts 9:26-27 and identify ways that Barnabas showed team care for Paul.

""26When he came to Jerusalem, he tried to join the disciples, but they were all afraid of him, not believing that he really was a disciple. 27But Barnabus took him and brought him to the apostles. He told them how Saul on his journey had seen the Lord and that the Lord had spoken to him, and how in Damascus he had preached fearlessly in the name of Jesus."

Barnabas' story reminds us that sometimes it takes a single leader to motivate the team towards caring for others and including new teammates. It's not easy to do this alone, but sometimes it is necessary.

Ask:
What would be your first reaction-to include or exclude Paul because of his questionable past?
How and what did Barnabas communicate to the larger team?
> *(He demonstrated acceptance by including him).*
How did Barnabas demonstrate care for the individual?
> *(He believed Paul and, more importantly, he believed in him.)*
What sacrifice do you think Barnabas and the rest of the team made in order to accept Paul?

Challenge students to approach their current team situation with the attitude of Barnabas. What can one individual do to improve the level of team care currently practiced? What personal sacrifice are you willing to make to accomplish this goal?

Ask:
Would a non-believer be impressed by the level of team care we currently demonstrate?
If we were serious about increasing team care, what would need to change?

"Mine Field" Activity
(adapted from Tom Heck at teachmeteamwork.com)

This activity will put the three principles involved in team care (communication, individual care and sacrifice) into practice. It will also give students the opportunity to evaluate their performance during the debriefing time.

Equipment:

- One boundary rope (70-100 feet)

- 50 objects for mines (tennis balls, etc.)

- Blindfolds (enough for half of the team)

- Objects to retrieve (one for each person on the team)

Instructions

Using the 70 feet of rope, create a boundary that is shaped more or less like a rectangle. Shape the rope irregularly on the long sides of the rectangle so the participants cannot follow the edge of the rope as a potential "path" to the other side. Spread out the 50+ obstacles inside the boundary in such a way that there are no straight pathways through the minefield. NOTE: During the actual activity, you may find the group has located an "easy" pathway that you didn't see beforehand. Allow yourself the option as the facilitator to rearrange the obstacles in the minefield.

Place the team's goals/desired outcomes at one end of the rectangle. Have the group start at the opposite end and travel through the minefield to pick them up and then return back through the minefield. Read the following scenario to the students:

The government has contracted our group to clear a dangerous minefield and retrieve sensitive documents from the other side. This minefield is located in a radioactive zone so we must wear eye protection at all times (blindfolds). Your job is to work in pairs to retrieve as many documents as you can.

Before the group actually starts (after they've read the instructions), warn them that a "communication breakdown" may occur during the activity. If this happens, people will not be allowed to communicate verbally. Don't tell them how long it will last (make it last a couple of minutes at the most).

Rules:

- The group must begin at the designated starting area.

- You must work in pairs. When one partner is inside the minefield, the other must remain outside. This person may travel anywhere else to assist their partner.

- People traveling through the minefield must wear protective eyewear (the blindfold). Vision may be used again after returning to the starting area.

- Partners can't touch their sightless partner while guiding them through the minefield.

- If anyone touches a landmine or the rope perimeter, they must return to the starting area and switch roles with their partner. If you have a document in your hand and touch a landmine or the perimeter rope, the document also must be returned.

- Only a sightless person who has successfully traveled through the minefield may handle/retrieve a document.

- Documents must be carried. They can't be thrown or handed off.

- Only one document may be carried per trip through the minefield.

- Participants may not alter the playing area, but the facilitator can change it.

To debrief, have students answer this Team Care Assessment on a scale from 1 (ineffective) to 10 (perfectly effective). This exercise can be very powerful. Be sure that you allow for honesty but also focus on team issues, not individual issues.

Based on how your team performed in this exercise, answer the following:

1. Direct Communication

Think about how your partner communicated with you during the Minefield activity. When you were in charge of the safety of the other person you were very careful to communicate well to that person. Direct communication is a great building block of team care.

_____ How well do you communicate to your teammates?

_____ How well do we communicate to each other?

_____ How important is it for you that our team communicates?

2. Value for the Individual

Every individual was essential to the success of this endeavor. You could not overlook someone's weaknesses or struggles during the initiative—you had to work together with them to overcome it. Every member of your team has something to contribute.

_____ How well do you value every individual on your team?

_____ How well does our team value each individual?

_____ How important is it to you that we value every individual on our team?

3. Sacrifice

Everyone must be willing to sacrifice for the sake of the team. It is often the missing component to achieving success. The biblical ideal for team care is caring for others MORE than you care for yourself.

_____ How well do you sacrifice for other team members?

_____ How well do we sacrifice as a team?

_____ How important is sacrifice to our team?

Close with a prayer for unity and an extra measure of love inside the group. A high performance team will care for each other to the nth degree, and no sacrifice will seem too small. Is this attitude possible among your team? Pray for God's Spirit to become alive and active inside each member to create extraordinary team care.

Lesson Summary:

- Leaders understand that great teams care deeply about each other.
- Team care requires direct communication.
- Team care requires valuing the individual.
- Team care requires sacrifice.

Lesson Seven

Increasing Team Care

Introduction:
Leaders understand that great teams care deeply about each other.

Going Public:
Do you think this team as a whole truly cares about each other? Why or why not?

Getting Focused:
1. Team Care Involves Direct _____

2. Team Care Shows Value for the _____

3. Team Care Requires _____

Growing Deeper:
Read Acts 9:26-27 and identify ways that Barnabas showed team care for Paul.

Barnabas' story reminds us that sometimes it takes a single leader to motivate the team to care for others and include new teammates. It's not easy to do this alone, but sometimes it is necessary.

1. Direct Communication
Think about how your partner communicated with you during the Minefield activity. When you were in charge of the safety of the other person, you were very careful to communicate well to that person. Direct communication is a great building block of team care.

_____ How well do you communicate to your teammates?

_____ How well do we communicate to each other?

_____ How important is it for you that our team communicates?

2. Value for the Individual
Every individual was essential to the success of this endeavor. You could not overlook someone's weaknesses or struggles during the initiative—you had to work with them to overcome it. Every member of your team has something to contribute.

_____ How well do you value every individual on your team?

_____ How well does our team value each individual?

_____ How important is it to you that we value every individual on our team?

3. Sacrifice
Everyone must be willing to sacrifice for the sake of the team. Sacrifice is often the missing component for achieving success. The biblical ideal for team care is caring for others MORE than you care for yourself.

_____ How well do you sacrifice for other team members?

_____ How well do we sacrifice as a team?

_____ How important is sacrifice to our team?

Lesson Summary:
- Leaders understand that great teams care deeply about each other.
- Team care requires direct communication.
- Team care requires valuing the individual.
- Team care requires sacrifice.

Lesson Eight

Inspiring Team Performance

Introduction:

Leaders motivate great teams to deliver great performances. Reaching peak performance as a team requires leaders to take a hard look at themselves. In order for them to be at their best, they must be willing to evaluate their performance and commit to making the necessary changes.

In this lesson, students will:

- Consider three key principles in creating team performance.
- Study the example of team performance by the Apostles in Acts 1.
- Analyze the team's weaknesses and strengths during a specific initiative.

Going Public:

Share what you learned from one of the following experiences:

1. A time when you performed less than your best
2. A time when you out-performed what you thought you could do

    (Think: at school, in sports, music recital, etc.)

Note: You're looking for the most honest answer possible. Challenge students to "go public" with their fears and emotions as they relay their own personal experiences.

Expert Opinions:

"If everyone is moving forward together, then success takes care of itself." *Henry Ford*

"Teamwork is a make or break situation. Either you help make it or the lack of it will break you." *Kris A Hiatt*

"No one can whistle a symphony. It takes a whole orchestra to play it." *H.E. Luccock*

"Alone we can do so little, together we can do so much." *Helen Keller*

"Two men were suggested: One of them was Joseph Barsabbas, known as Justus, and the other was Matthias. Then they all prayed, "Lord, you know what everyone is like! Show us the one you have chosen." *Acts 1:23-24 (CEV)*

Getting Focused:

To introduce this lesson to students, have students focus on the quote below.

"A team has one heartbeat."

Ask:
What does this mean?
What is the heartbeat of our team? Is it irregular? Too fast? Too slow? Healthy? Explain.

Optional Activity

A second option is to show a clip from Hoosiers starring Gene Hackman as a basketball coach in Indiana during the 1950s with an unorthodox approach to the game. In this clip, his team fights for the state championship in the final 19 seconds.

Hoosiers (1986)

Final scene on DVD at the state championship, Hickory vs. Indiana University (Hoosiers)

Ask:
What principles do you learn about a team achieving peak performance from this clip?
How would you define "peak performance"?

Say something like:
Leaders know a team is designed to accomplish a goal or a mission. Without a purpose, a team is merely a group of people sharing space. Having a leader is pointless. However, when you establish the goal, it galvanizes a team to action. For us to be at our best we must be willing to give whatever it takes toward our goal.

Think about some of the activities and efforts your student ministry has experienced in the past six months in outreach, evangelism, Bible study groups, small groups, prayer ministry, etc. Make a specific list on a large sheet of paper, but focus your list on no more than three activities.

For example:

1. High school outreach night March 12

2. Small group ministry, April-June

3. Prayer Ministry started last month

Ask:
What were some of our goals for these events/ministries?
How would you rate our performance in each of these events in terms of our ability to reach our goals?
What is needed to reach a higher level of performance as a team?

Encourage students to be specific in their responses. For example, what is needed in terms of: attitude, resources, time together, navigating obstacles, team care, goals, etc.

Share the following illustration:

On June 27, 1976 a group terrorists hijacked an Air France plane heading from Tel Aviv, Israel to Paris, France. The plane carried 248 passengers and a crew of 12. The hijackers diverted the plane to Entebbe Airport in Uganda, Africa. The terrorists demanded the release of 40 Palestinians held by Israel. They released all the passengers except for 103 Jewish hostages. They set July 4 as the deadline to release the Palestinians or the hijackers would kill the hostages.

The Israeli government approved a secret mission to rescue the Jewish hostages. A team of 29 Special Forces members began training for this operation. They interviewed the released passengers to gain valuable information on the situation. They practiced their surprise assault using a scale model of the building holding the hostages.

On the night of July 3, a British Airways plane landed to refuel at the airport. Four large C-130 cargo planes followed close behind it undetected by radar. When the cargo doors opened, a black Mercedes and four Land Rovers headed to the terminal building. The convoy looked similar to the one used by the Ugandan president, a convenient decoy.

The assault lasted 30 minutes and resulted in successful rescue of the hostages. Casualties included six terrorists, three hostages and an Israeli commander. Today, armed forces around the world use the Raid on Entebbe as an example of superb team performance.

Ask:
What did the Israeli army do to ensure success?
        (They interviewed released hostages. They practiced on a scale model.)
What do you think is a key element of "superb team performance"?
How much were the Israeli special forces willing to sacrifice for success?

Team Performance is affected by three key components:

1. Team Performance Requires <u>Winning Attitude</u>

What separates a great team from others is a winning attitude. Accomplishing great things does not happen by accident. It requires focus and effort. A team that focuses on winning is simply able to accomplish more. Leaders have a strong belief in what God can do through His people. Their winning attitude energizes and inspires the people around them so that they can accomplish their goal in extraordinary ways.

2. Team Performance Requires <u>100 % Effort</u>

Teams are at their strongest when each member is giving everything they've got. Leaders are especially sensitive to weaker members' struggles and they seek to help them overcome. Every person must be committed to the mission of the team and do his or her part. When commitment waivers, effort quickly falls off and the results are devastating.

3. Team Performance Requires <u>Exceeding Expectations</u>

A team is only as strong as its strongest members. Great teams and powerful leaders are not willing to accept the status quo. They want more from themselves and from those around them. Teams that are top performers are those who are willing to exceed their expectations and attempt great things for God.

Say something like:
Remember that teambuilding is an ongoing process. You will never fully arrive as a team. Continue to expect the best from each other. Guard against complacency. God will do amazing things through those teams who are willing to focus on growth, as we see in the story of the early church in Acts.

Growing Deeper:
The disciples faced a lag in team performance when they lost a team member, Judas. We can learn several principles of team performance through the story of how they decided to replace him.

Read Acts 1:12-26 and identify ways the early church demonstrated outstanding team performance.

"12Then they returned to Jerusalem from the hill called the Mount of Olives, a Sabbath day's walk from the city. 13When they arrived, they went upstairs to the room where they were staying. Those present were Peter, John, James and Andrew; Philip and Thomas, Bartholomew and Matthew; James son of Alphaeus and Simon the Zealot, and Judas son of James. 14They all joined together constantly in prayer, along with the women and Mary the mother of Jesus, and with his brothers. 15In those days Peter stood up among the believers (a group numbering about a hundred and twenty) 16and said, "Brothers, the Scripture had to be fulfilled which the Holy Spirit spoke long ago through the mouth of David concerning Judas, who served as guide for those who arrested Jesus– 17he was one of our number and shared in this ministry." 18(With the reward he got for his wickedness, Judas bought a field; there he fell headlong, his body burst open and all his intestines spilled out. 19Everyone in Jerusalem heard about this, so they called that field in their language Akeldama, that is, Field of Blood.) 20"For," said Peter, "it is written in the book of Psalms, " 'May his place be deserted; let there be no one to dwell in it,' and, " 'May another take his place of leadership.' 21Therefore it is necessary to choose one of the men who have been with us the whole time the Lord Jesus went in and out among us, 22beginning from John's baptism to the time when Jesus was taken up from us. For one of these must become a witness with us of his resurrection." 23So they proposed two men: Joseph called Barsabbas (also known as Justus) and Matthias. 24Then they prayed, "Lord, you know everyone's heart. Show us which of these two you have chosen 25to take over this apostolic ministry, which Judas left to go where he belongs." 26Then they cast lots, and the lot fell to Matthias; so he was added to the eleven apostles."

The suggested principles from this passage include:

> They lived together in the same room for a time.
>
> They prayed together.
>
> The studied the Bible together.
>
> They brought their findings to the church.
>
> They suggested a selection process.
>
> They prayed for God's will in selecting a replacement.
>
> They followed through on their plan.

"All Hands on Deck" Activity

(adapted from Tom Heck at teachmeteamwork.com)

Equipment:

> Wooden blocks
>
> Boundary ropes

Instructions

Give the team enough blocks (life boats) so that all but two or three participants have a block. Set the boundary ropes as "starting and finish lines" at least 100 feet apart. (Be sure it's farther than your team standing hand-to-hand holding their arms up in a 'T'...making them pass at least 5 blocks before successfully crossing.) These ropes mark the boundaries of a shark-infested sea.

Describe the following scenario to your team:

Your expedition team has had a successful journey of discovery so far off the coast of India. You have seen great things and are returning to your home country to tell your tale. However, you have found a new, faster way home, but it means having to cross a shark infested sea in lifeboats. You have built a specific number of lifeboats to get your team across. You will need to move the boats while working your team across the sea. Watch out for pirates!

Rules:

- The team must remain in contact with each other at all times

- The team must remain in contact with all blocks at all times

- If a block is left unattended, the pirates (facilitators) will take it. The team will have to press on with a limited number of blocks.

- If anyone touches the sea (floor) the entire team must start over.

- The initiative is over when the team reaches the opposite shore (finish line).

Debrief this initiative by answering the questions below:

What were some of the obstacles we faced as a team?
How many obstacles were internal to the team (attitudes, etc.) and how many were external (circumstances)?
Based on your performance in this initiative, what are the strengths of your team?
What are the weaknesses of your team?

Close this lesson by giving your team a personal word of encouragement about their team performance to date. Point out some specific positive behaviors and attitudes you have witnessed since you began this emphasis on leadership training. Cast a vision for their continued development as leaders-let the group in on some of the goals you have for them in their future. After a few minutes, divide the team into threes to spend some time sharing one or two ways they have seen the team change since beginning this leadership training. Close in a time of prayer.

Lesson Summary:

- A great team has a winning attitude.

- All team members must give 100%.

- A great team must exceed expectations.

From The Student Guide

Lesson Eight

Inspiring Team Performance

Introduction:
Leaders motivate great teams to deliver great performances. In order for leaders to be at their best, they must be willing to evaluate their performance and commit to making the necessary changes.

Going Public:
Share what you learned from one of the following experiences: (Think: at school, in sports, music recital, etc.)

1. A time when you performed less than your best.

2. A time when you out-performed your expectations.

Getting Focused:
"A team has one heartbeat."

1. Team performance requires _____ _____ .

2. Team performance requires _____ _____ .

3. Team performance requires _____ _____ .

Growing Deeper:
Read Acts 1:12-26 and identify ways the early church demonstrated outstanding team performance.

They lived together in the same room for a time.

They prayed together.

The studied the Bible together.

They brought their findings to the church.

They suggested a selection process.

They prayed for God's will in selecting a replacement.

They followed through on their plan.

Lesson Summary:
- A great team has a winning attitude.
- All team members must give 100%.
- A great team must exceed expectation

54

55

Section Five:
Best Practices in Student Leadership

Demystifying Leadership

High school students tend to think of leadership as a position; captain of the football team, student government president or first chair in the band. In students' minds, natural selection determines leadership, not training. A recent study interviewed high schoolers and businessmen about leadership and found that 80% of high schoolers said that leaders are born, not made. However, 80% of business leaders said that leaders are made, not born. This study points directly to the fact that students believe that leadership is for a select few.

If we want to get students interested in leadership we need to demystify leadership. We need to show them that each one of them can be a person of influence in the schools, churches and families. How do we demystify leadership? By teaching, molding and equipping them with basic leadership principles. They need to understand that leadership is just a set of principles that we apply to any given situation.

At LeaderTreks we call this first step to becoming a leader - Leadership Learned

Leadership Learned

Leadership Learned is the first stage of leadership development. In this stage, students learn a set of leadership principles. It's easy for us to assume that students know how to lead-but it's not so. It's true they know how to influence peers, but what they don't know is how to create a vision and take a group of followers toward that goal.

Leadership must be taught. At LeaderTreks, we focus on ten key leadership principles that we feel are foundational to leadership development (available at www.leadertreks.com). By teaching students these skills we can prepare them to take on leadership roles.

Let's take a look at how you might equip students with one of these leadership principles: Strategic Planning (see the lesson entitled "What Are the Tasks of a Leader?" in this resource). It would be easy for you to sit down one day and plan everything for the upcoming youth group even that week. What if, instead of doing this on your own, you brought three students alongside you with the intention of teaching them the leadership principle of Strategic Planning?

First, you would teach them that in Strategic Planning you have to:

- Set a Goal

- Gather Needed Materials and Resources

- Cast vision

- Navigate obstacles

- Evaluate Progress

Then you would mentor them through the process of how you do each one of these in planning for the upcoming youth group. Together the four of you would go through the process of strategic planning. Consider giving this a try the next time you plan a student ministry activity and help students understand leadership is not beyond their reach.

Debriefing Leadership Experiences

As many of you know, an effective student leadership development program needs to focus on the two sides of leadership development; solid leadership training and real leadership experiences where students play the role of a leader.

The leadership experience must become transformational in students' lives. In order to do so, we must first understand that there is more to a great leadership experience than just doing the experience. Debriefing and mentoring of student leaders need to be part of the process. Jesus was the master of this as He worked with His disciples. In Luke 10:1-20, Jesus sent His followers on a mission trip. When they returned, Jesus sat with the disciples and debriefed the experience with them. Jesus knew that His followers would face these trials again; debriefing the experience would help them in the future. We must do the same with our student leaders. Whenever leadership experiences happen, be intentional and set aside some time to debrief and help students apply the lessons to their lives.

This is the LeaderTreks process for debriefing a leadership experience:

1. Uncover the truth.

Ask questions that will lead students to uncover truths about the leadership experience. They should be able to identify strengths and areas that need improvement. Make sure to celebrate the wins and to be honest about what needs to change. In this first step, don't do much talking; just ask questions and let students process what took place. You might ask two main questions: What was the problem you were facing? How did you feel when you were facing this problem? These two questions should be enough to help students uncover the truth about the event and expose what leadership skills need to be improved.

2. Identify areas for improvement.

In this step, you play the role of mentor, a person who helps students understand what they have experienced and how they can grow from it. Students have uncovered the areas of their leadership that needs work. The experience is still fresh in their minds and you come alongside and mentor them as they make changes to improve. You are still going to want to ask questions, but here you are also going to want to teach. This is a great opportunity to turn failures into wins by creating action steps to change.

3. Apply the leadership lesson to life

Students will now see how their leadership needs to improve, but you can take it a step further by asking them to apply what they have learned to their daily lives. It's not our goal to develop leaders just for youth group events but to equip students for longterm leadership in the kingdom. The questions are simple: How does this apply to your life at school, in your family and with your friends? Ask students to be specific and ask them if you can hold them accountable, as that will make a big difference.

Leadership experiences for students are powerful. They want to do a good job and they want to be effective as leaders. When you debrief with them, they understand that it's okay to make a mistake and they know that you support them. A student leader who has a mentor and friends who support them will do great things for the kingdom of God.

Implementing the LeaderTreks Model

Most youth workers don't know how to create student leaders. Student leadership is not about doing menial tasks at meetings. It's not about teaching students to think and talk just like you. It's about training students to become leaders for the kingdom who make a difference. It's about risk taking and the kind of failure that leads to success. Student leadership can be the ingredient to take students to the next level of spiritual development.

LeaderTreks has been pursuing the mission of developing leaders to fulfill the Great Commission for many years. Through the process of teaching and challenging students, we have created a model of leadership development that has the power to revolutionize your ministry.

There are four stages of leadership development including leadership learned, leadership experienced, leadership challenged and leadership evaluated. You will also discover what role staff can play and the outcomes you can expect in students' lives.

Leadership learned is the first stage of leadership development. In this stage, students learn a set of leadership principles. At LeaderTreks, we focus on ten key leadership principles that we feel are foundational to leadership development (see www.leadertreks.com). By teaching students these skills, we can prepare them to take on leadership roles. It is important to teach skills that are substantive. Students are not motivated by a watered down version of leadership development. They want tools they can use to make a difference.

The staff role at this stage is to **model** these leadership principles. As a leader, your students must see you as an example they can emulate. They need to see you learning and growing as a leader, taking risks and pursuing excellence. This role also requires you to have a good relationship with students. Students will learn more from those they know and trust. At this stage, the desired outcome is for the student to know and understand a set of **leadership principles** such as those taught in Leadership 365.

The second stage of leadership development is leadership experienced. It is here that students are given leadership roles of true importance. The temptation for many youth workers is to hold onto the true leadership opportunities and never allow students to make decisions that really matter. Students need to be able to make decisions that will affect the rest of the group. This allows the student to feel the full weight of leadership when their decisions could lead to failure for others.

The experience of leadership should take place in an environment that is closely guarded by the adult staff. This will free students to take risks in their leadership development. The staff's role is **empowering** students to feel safe and be successful. It is never a good idea to put students in a position where they are set up to fail. Be sure to allow room for failure, but don't create it. The outcome for students at this level is for them to take **ownership** of the experience. Their actions will determine the success or failure of the mission.

After students learn leadership principles, they are placed in leadership roles. The natural outcome of experiencing leadership comes as students learn to face challenges. **Leadership challenged represents the third stage of LeaderTreks' leadership development model.** Students need to experience the stresses and struggles of leadership while under direction of adults who care about their growth. The temptation for staff is to step in and rescue students when they face challenge for the first time. It can be very uncomfortable for adult staff, especially volunteers in your program, to watch students as they experience challenge.

The role for staff at this stage is to **motivate** students. There is a fine line between rescuing and motivating. One bench mark we use is watching how students are responding to the challenge. If students are processing and working through the struggle, it is important to let them continue. When a student is so overwhelmed by the challenge that they stop learning from the experience it is vital to step in and help them overcome the challenge. Our desire for students at this level is to experience and overcome **struggle**.

The final stage of leadership development, leadership evaluated, is a key component to solidifying and applying the lessons that students are learning. We have found that evaluation is often overlooked by youth workers because they are not comfortable pursing it with students or don't know how to use it in their program. It is important to create an evaluation environment that is peer-to-peer and not adult-to-student. When students learn to confront each other and overcome obstacles to teamwork by speaking truth into each other's lives, true leadership development takes place.

The role of the staff at this stage is to facilitate the **evaluation** process. Students have a tendency to take evaluation to one extreme or the other. Sometimes evaluation turns into a punishment session for the weakest member of the team. Other times students are too afraid to bring up hard issues in front of the whole group. The goal is to create an atmosphere of love and care. Staff may have to work hard to create a balanced evaluation environment but it is well worth the effort. The desired outcome for students at this level is to see measurable **growth**. People grow from honest evaluation and it motivates them to move forward as a leader.

As a youth worker you have the ability to create an effective program for your students. By applying the LeaderTreks model to your program you can create a healthy environment that will produce powerful leaders.

Evaluating Your Leadership Model

Leadership development needs to be a foundational part of any student ministry program. Those in youth ministry need to realize that the church is only one generation away from having no leaders. Students today must be equipped with the skills to lead into the future. Many in youth ministry feel the pressure to teach leadership skills but don't know what it takes to empower students to become leaders. LeaderTreks uses a time-tested, proven program to move students to new heights of leadership ability.

- Leadership Learned

- Leadership Experienced

- Leadership Challenged

- Leadership Evaluated

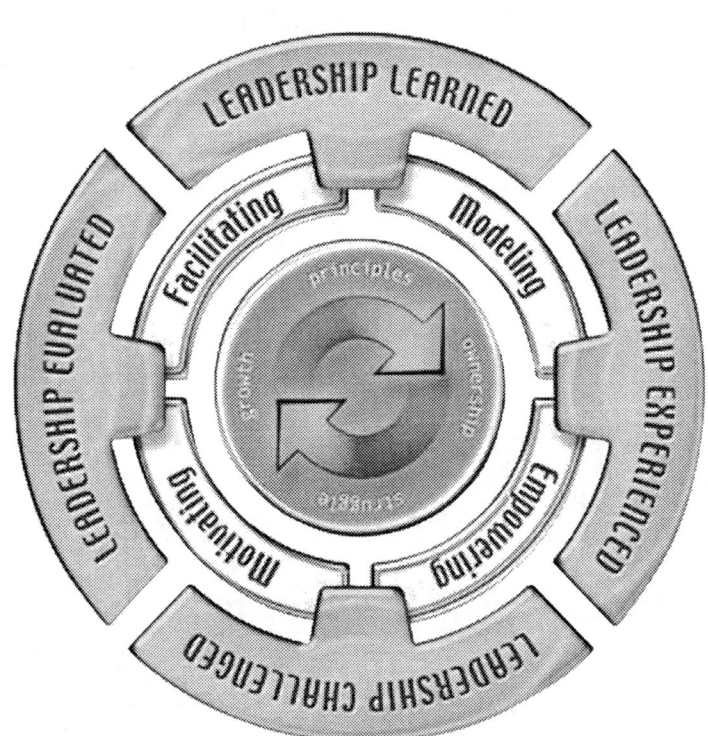

The LeaderTreks leadership development model is designed to continue in a cycle of growth for students. Students constantly experience the various stages of leadership development. This tool can be useful to many youth workers looking for a process to grow student leaders in their ministry. To apply this model to your youth ministry think about these steps.

1. What principles of leadership do you want to teach your students?

You need to prepare your students for the leadership roles they will fulfill. If you need a place to start contact us at LeaderTreks and ask about our resources.

2. What leadership experiences can you offer in your youth ministry?

Remember to find experiences that offer true leadership challenges. Possibilities for student leadership include planning and running a missions trip or heading up a ministry in the church.

3. What is your plan for challenging your students?

You will need to educate your volunteer staff on your plan. Be sure to leave room for students to struggle.

4. How will you evaluate your student leaders so they can grow from this process?

At LeaderTreks, we use evaluation every day when we are on a leadership development trip. Youth workers might want to have regular evaluation meetings with the student leadership team.

Even though the road to developing an effective leadership development program can be long and difficult, it is well worth the effort. The kingdom is in need of young people who are equipped with the skills necessary to lead the church. We believe that every student can learn to be a better leader. We also believe that by making leadership development a foundation of your ministry, you will be able to challenge and grow students in ways you never have before.

The Balanced Leadership Development Program

What's the first thing that comes to your mind when you hear "student leadership"? Many think, "Another meeting with students" and the rest think, "Put the students in charge." Actually both are right-a good student leadership program has both training and experience tied together as key components. The problem is that we often go with one or the other.

To have an effective leadership development program, you need to focus on the two sides of leadership development (see lesson Leadership Involves Being and Doing in this resource). You must have solid leadership training for students, and you need to give students real leadership experience where they play active leadership roles. When these two sides of leadership development are in balance, you have a solid student leadership development program. When you concentrate on only one aspect, you get a program that is out of balance.

How do you balance the training with experience?

Let's look at a case study - youth pastor Bob wants his student leadership team to run this year's winter retreat. For the last several years, he has taken care of all the details including the games and the spiritual content of the weekend. He realizes this retreat is a perfect opportunity for his student leaders to step up and breathe some new life into an old activity.

The retreat is over a long weekend in February due to parent/teacher conferences. The church has a long-standing relationship with a camp that is close to a ski resort. Pastor Bob sits down with his team in late October to give them the challenge of coming up with the winter retreat program.

Bob already has a good leadership experience line-up in the retreat itself. Now he needs to add some pre-experience training to make the leadership development effective. When he lays out the challenge for students to lead the retreat, he requires students to commit to several training lessons. Students are all in.

At the first training session, students are excited because they think they are going to be dreaming up new games and deciding how much time they get to ski. However, Bob has some different ideas. He first starts with a dream session on "how we want to be different after the retreat." Students are puzzled - what does this discussion have to do with being the leaders of the retreat? "Everything," Bob explains. Leaders of retreats don't just think about what is going to happen; they think about how people are going to grow spiritually. We don't go on retreats to ski but to retreat and focus on lives on God. Bob goes on to explain that by deciding what outcome we want, we are able to pick activities that help us reach those goals. Now that the students are thinking differently; they start a white board session on the spiritual needs of fellow students. This first training session ends differently. Students are transformed from thinking about activities to thinking about how the activities can help them minister to other students.

At the second training session, students are focused on spiritual outcomes for the retreat and start to plan activities that will attract students and help them reach their goals. Bob wants to use this training session to teach his student leaders about strategic planning. He knows their first thoughts are to choose activities, and the last thing on their minds is what it will take to accomplish them. So, as activities are chosen, Bob asks students to make lists of all needed material and equipment for each activity. He also asks the students to assign one member of the team to be the leader of the activity. As the second training session comes to an end, Bob hears students say things like, "Man, a lot goes into this-who did this before?" Bob thinks to himself, "I love student leadership."

At the third training session, Bob knows he still has lots to cover and wants to make sure his student leaders get the most out of the experience. In the coming weeks, his student leaders will make the announcement in youth group about the winter retreat. He has decided to focus this training on helping students cast the vision for the event to fellow students. Bob understands that announcing the time, place and cost will only excite a few students, so he asks his student leaders for help. "Why are we having this event and how will you describe it to your friends?"

After a short but productive discussion, Bob asks one student to stand up in front of the team and give a practice announcement. With much excitement, the student stands up and tells the group about all the cool things that are going to happen on the retreat but never mentions the potential of the retreat to have an impact on student's spiritual lives. Bob asks the team if the student hit all the bases. They quickly realize how hard it is to communicate what is in their hearts as opposed to just what is in their heads. Bob breaks the team into groups of two to work on casting the vision for the retreat.

The student leaders have learned a lot-the process wasn't actually what they thought it would be but they have learned a ton about how leaders operate. Through this process they set the goals for the retreat, strategically plan for all the events and prepare to cast a vision to fellow students.

LeaderTreks, your partner in leadership development

LeaderTreks wants to be your resource for leadership development. We partner with youth workers to develop student leaders. We have three main categories of ministry resources, specifically designed for student leadership development: trips, training events, and curriculum.

Leadership Focused Trips

We provide missions and wilderness trips that engage student leaders.

- Missions Trips: LeaderTreks provides challenging, intentional, leadership-focused missions experiences.

- Wilderness Trips: We harness the environment of the wilderness to develop students' leadership potential.

- Adventure Trips: A unique combination trip that merges the best of a missions trip and a wilderness trip. A popular choice.

Three-Day Leadership Training Events:

An event designed to give your students the tools they need to become leaders.

- Each event is formatted to fit into a weekend retreat schedule, with four powerful sessions that engage students.

- You host the event. Our full time staff will come to your location and do the rest.

- Topics include Foundations of Leadership, Team Building Basics, or IVision, among others.

Leadership Curriculum:

LeaderTreks curriculum resources are designed to help you develop student leaders.

- Leadership Assessments: LeaderTreks provides seven unique, student-oriented assessments, including leadership style, character, and spiritual gifts—all designed just for students.

- Becoming a Leader: This series provides youth workers with a convenient method for continuing the process of leadership development throughout the year.

- Field Guide: Our Field Guides are time tested trip curricula designed to introduce students to Bible study, prayer journaling, and growth journaling.

Check out our website or call for more information on any of our resources.

www.leadertreks.com   1-877-502-0699